I Never Knew That
About

THE LAKE DISTRICT

CHRISTOPHER WINN

I Never Knew That
About

THE LAKE DISTRICT

ILLUSTRATIONS BY
Mai Osawa

EBURY
PRESS

1 3 5 7 9 10 8 6 4 2

Published in 2010 by Ebury Press, an imprint of Ebury Publishing

A Random House Group Company

Text © Christopher Winn 2010
Illustrations © Mai Osawa 2010

The Random House Group Limited Reg. No. 954009

Addresses for companies within the Random House Group can be found at
www.randomhouse.co.uk

A CIP catalogue record for this book is available from the British Library

The Random House Group Limited supports The Forest Stewardship
Council (FSC), the leading international forest certification organisation. All our titles
that are printed on Greenpeace approved FSC certified paper carry the FSC logo. Our
paper procurement policy can be found at www.rbooks.co.uk/environment

Mixed Sources
Product group from well-managed
forests and other controlled sources
www.fsc.org   Cert no. TT-COC-2139
© 1996 Forest Stewardship Council

To buy books by your favourite authors and register for offers visit
www.rbooks.co.uk

Series designed by Peter Ward

Typeset by Palimpsest Book Production Limited,
Grangemouth, Stirlingshire
Printed and bound in Great Britain by
CPI Mackays, Chatham, ME5 8TD

ISBN: 978 0 09 193314 2

For Maki

Contents

Preface

'*No part of the world possesses so many charms for the contemplative mind as the admirable scenery of our English Lake District.*'

So wrote Lorenzo Tuvar in his *Tales and Legends of the English Lakes* in 1852, confirming the view of poets and painters before him and of innumerable artists, thinkers and visitors since.

In fact, the Lake District inspired its very own style of Romantic poetry, as fashioned by the Lake Poets, Samuel Taylor Coleridge, Robert Southey and William Wordsworth, who wrote their finest verse while under the influence of the Lake District's striking combination of lake and mountain, water and sky.

So superbly did the Lake Poets capture the beauty of the Lakes, that thousands came to see it for themselves, threatening the very beauty they had come to admire. First Wordsworth, then Ruskin and finally Canon Rawnsley fought to save their beloved landscape, and it was largely the desire to preserve the Lake District that brought about the founding of the National Trust. The Trust now owns over one-quarter of the Lake District.

This compact corner of north-west England claims far more than its fair share of England's natural treasures. The Lake District National Park is England's largest national park, possessing all the land in England over 3,000 feet (914 m), with England's highest mountains, highest passes and steepest roads, biggest and deepest lakes, largest population of rare red squirrels and England's only golden eagles.

Man has also contributed to the scenery with picturesque packhorse bridges, tiny churches, stone cottages and luscious gardens.

People come to the Lake District to ride on the oldest steamboats in the world, to see the home of Peter Rabbit and Mrs Tiggywinkle, to discover the places they have read about in *Swallows and Amazons*, to seek out that famous 'host of daffodils' and to pit themselves against the very mountains that gave birth to the sport of rock climbing. The lakes may not be the biggest or deepest in the world, and the mountains may not be the highest or most awesome but, as Wordsworth said, 'they are surpassed by none'.

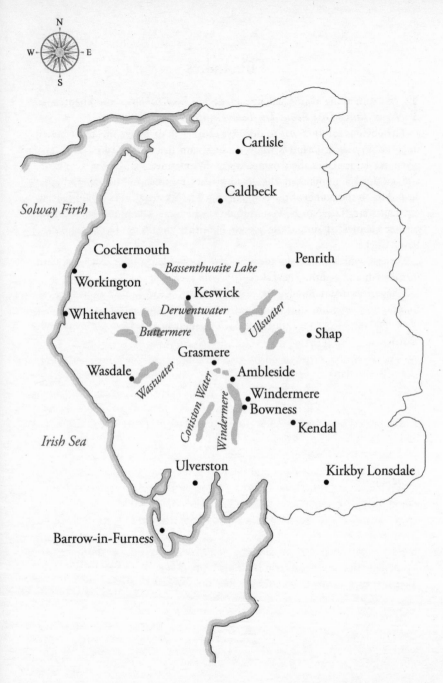

The Lakes

It was something of a challenge to decide how to order the chapters in *I Never Knew That About The Lake District.*

The obvious solution was to devote a chapter to each lake but this resulted in some very short chapters when dealing with the smaller lakes. So I have given the larger lakes their own chapter, Windermere, Ullswater, Coniston, and grouped a number of the smaller lakes together in the same chapter according to the points of the compass, i.e. The Western Lakes, The Far Eastern Lakes etc. The North-Western Lakes, which are more numerous, I have further subdivided into those joined by either the River Derwent, or the River Cocker.

Furness, which is distinct and was once part of Lancashire, I have divided into North and South. The Lakeland Coast speaks for itself.

I have featured a number of places, Carlisle, Kendal, Barrow-in-Furness, that do not lie within the boundaries of the Lake District National Park, but are nonetheless close to, influenced by, or generally associated with the Lake District.

THE CENTRAL LAKES

WILLIAM WORDSWORTH ✦ WORDSWORTH COUNTRY ✦
GRASMERE ✦ RYDAL WATER ✦ ELTERWATER ✦ AMBLESIDE

William Wordsworth, the doyen of the Lake Poets

Wordsworth Country

A Poet's Inspiration

WORDSWORTH COUNTRY, the area of the Lake District around Grasmere and Rydal Water, is so called because it was where the poet William Wordsworth lived and wrote for over 50 years. Here is the scenery that immersed him and inspired his romantic poetry, the poetry that was the greatest influence on, perhaps even the creation of, the way we see and treat the Lake District today. No study of the Lake District can really be appreciated without at least a brief look first at Wordsworth and Wordsworth Country.

William Wordsworth
(1770–1850)

WILLIAM WORDSWORTH, the most renowned of the Lakeland poets, was born on the edge of the Lake District in Cockermouth, spending most his childhood there or in his mother's home town of Penrith. After his mother died he attended Hawkshead Grammar School for eight years, during which time he wandered far and wide through the countryside of the southern lakes developing a love and appreciation for the beauties of the Lake District. He later went to St John's College, Cambridge, and then spent some years exploring the Continent.

In 1799 Wordsworth and his sister Dorothy undertook a tour of the Lake District in the company of SAMUEL TAYLOR COLERIDGE, whom they had met a few years earlier while staying in the Quantock Hills in Somerset, and with whom Wordsworth had first toured the Lake District in 1797.

The Lake Poets

Passing by Grasmere they came across a small, abandoned 17th-century inn called the DOVE AND OLIVE BOUGH, set in the hillside at Town End, five minutes' walk from the centre of GRASMERE village. They fell in love with it, and in December 1799 Wordsworth and Dorothy moved into their first Lakeland home, calling it DOVE COTTAGE. Coleridge took up residence nearby at Greta Hall in Keswick, and was joined there shortly afterwards by their mutual friend ROBERT SOUTHEY. THE LAKE POETS, as they became known, were gathered.

Dove Cottage

The lovely cottage in the guardian nook
  Hath stirred me greatly with
    its own dear brook,
   Its own small pasture,
    almost its own sky!
     WILLIAM WORDSWORTH

DOVE COTTAGE was a surprisingly modest abode for a man of Wordsworth's stature, but he lived here for eight years and here wrote much of his greatest poetry, 'Ode to Duty', 'The Excursion', 'The Prelude', and 'Intimations of Immortality'. From the moment he and Dorothy arrived Dove Cottage became a social hub, always bursting with an assortment of poets and artists, many of them staying for days even though there was hardly room for the two of them. Coleridge came over from Keswick and would be a permanent fixture sometimes for weeks. Southey often came too, and the shy, sickly author THOMAS DE QUINCEY, who so adored Dove Cottage that he bought it for himself after Wordsworth left, and lived there for ten years.

How they all fitted in is a mystery, and it only got worse in 1802 when Wordsworth got married in Yorkshire to MARY HUTCHINSON, whom he had known at school in Penrith, and brought her home to Dove Cottage. It all proved too much for Dorothy, who locked herself in her room and sobbed with hysterics for hours. The first three of Wordsworth's five children were all born at Dove Cottage.

When SIR WALTER SCOTT came to stay he found Dove Cottage so lacking in certain comforts that he would climb out of his bedroom window and sneak off to the SWAN INN up the road for a fortifier. Scott's subterfuge came to light when he and his host went to the Swan to hire a pony and the landlord insisted on ushering them into Scott's 'usual' seat by the window, expressing consternation that Scott had taken him surprise by arriving earlier than normal.

Whenever the cottage was full, Wordsworth would take himself out into the garden to write, and the maelstrom seemed to work for him. Some of his finest lines emerged as he sat or paced under the trees, shouting above the hubbub: 'I wandered lonely as a cloud' or 'My heart leaps up when I behold a rainbow in the sky' or 'The child is father of the man' . . .

Today it is possible, in clement weather, to walk in the wild gardens of Dove Cottage where Wordsworth wrote his immortal lines. The cottage was acquired by the Wordsworth Trust in 1890 and opened the following year as a museum in his memory, and is largely unchanged since Wordsworth and his family lived there. The Wordsworth Museum is next door.

Swan Inn

Allan Bank

By 1808 Dove Cottage had become quite seriously too small to contain Wordsworth's burgeoning family, which consisted of not just his wife, three children and sister Dorothy, but also his sister-in-law Sara and permanent house guests de Quincey and Coleridge. Wordsworth swallowed his pride and moved them all into a larger house called ALLAN BANK at the foot of a craggy hill on the other side of Grasmere, which he had previously described as an eyesore. Two more children arrived in the two years they spent at Allan Bank, after which they fell out with the landlord over his failure to have their smoking chimneys attended to, and they moved on to the Old Rectory opposite the church in Grasmere.

In 1833 DR THOMAS ARNOLD, headmaster of Rugby School, rented Allan Bank while building himself a summer home near Ambleside, and later, in 1915, Allan Bank was bought by CANON RAWNSLEY, founder of the National Trust, who left it to the Trust. It is currently privately let and not open to the public.

Old Rectory

The Wordsworths' time at the OLD RECTORY was not a happy one. The house was cold and damp and two of their children, Thomas and Catherine, died there in 1812.

Rydal Mount

In 1813 Wordworth and his surviving brood made their final move, to RYDAL MOUNT, set on a hillside above the church at Rydal, rented from Lady le Fleming of Rydal Hall. Here he laid out the spacious gardens which he called his 'office', and built himself a 'writing hut', in truth a bench with a bit of roof, from where he could see both Windermere and Rydal Water.

In 1843 Wordsworth was appointed Poet Laureate, on the death of his friend Robert Southey who had held the position for 30 years.

Wordsworth also bought a small field next to the churchyard, with a thought to build a guest-house on it, but after his beloved daughter Dora died of tuberculosis in 1847 he renamed it DORA'S FIELD and planted hundreds of daffodils in her memory.

One evening in 1850 Wordsworth went out for a long walk and caught a cold, and he died at Rydal Mount of pleurisy a few days later, on St George's Day, 23 April, the day of Shakespeare's passing.

Rydal Mount was acquired by Wordsworth's great-great-granddaughter Mary in 1969, and has been open to the public ever since. Dora's Field belongs to the National Trust.

Wordsworth's Grave

Wordsworth was buried in the churchyard of ST OSWALD'S in Grasmere, and was later joined by his wife Mary when she died in 1859. Their simple headstone lies within sound of the River Rothay, beneath one of the yew trees Wordsworth himself had planted there, and the grave has become one of the most visited literary shrines in the world. As Matthew Arnold wrote:

> Keep fresh the grass upon his grave,
> O Rotha, with thy living wave!
> Sing him thy best, for few or none
> Hear thy voice right, now he has gone.

Nearby are buried Wordsworth's sister Dorothy, four of his children, Dora, William, Thomas and Catherine, his sister-in-law Sara and Samuel Taylor Coleridge's eldest son Hartley.

River Rothay

Wordsworth Country watered by the RIVER ROTHAY, which rises at 1,500 ft (457 m) up in the high fells above Grasmere, passes by DUNMAIL RAISE, then flows through GRASMERE and RYDAL WATER, past AMBLESIDE and out into Windermere beside GALAVA ROMAN FORT.

Dunmail Raise

DUNMAIL RAISE sits on the high point where the road north from Grasmere (A591) passes from the old county of Westmorland into Cumberland and begins to drop down towards Thirlmere. In AD 945 there was a battle here between DUNMAIL, the LAST KING OF CUMBRIA, and Alfred the Great's grandson KING EDMUND THE ELDER. Dunmail was killed by Edmund himself, who afterwards ordered Dunmail's warriors to gather together rocks and place them over the body of their dead king, forming a large cairn that remains there to this day.

Grasmere

Focal point of the area described by Wordsworth as 'the loveliest spot that man hath found', GRASMERE, the lake, is 1 mile (1.6 km) long, ½ mile (800

m) wide and 75 ft (23 m) deep. There is a small, wooded island in the middle to where Wordsworth would row for fishing and picnics with his sister Dorothy. Nowadays the island is privately owned and closed to the public, although it can be viewed from a rowing boat or canoe – powered boats are banned on Grasmere.

Grasmere Village

The most popular village in the Lake District thanks to Wordsworth's grave, GRASMERE, the village, is geared for tourists but nonetheless has some hidden charms.

The 13th-century church of St Oswald, where the Wordsworths lie buried in the churchyard, serves as parish church for the three villages of Grasmere, Rydal and Langdale, each village having its own separate gateway into the churchyard. Beside one of these gateways is a small building from 1630, which was once the village school where Wordsworth, his wife

and his sister all taught. Today it houses SARAH NELSON'S GRASMERE GINGERBREAD SHOP.

Across the road from the church is CHURCH STILE, a beautiful pink 17th-century cottage with bulging walls that was at one time ROBERT NEWTON'S INN, where Wordsworth and his fellow poet Samuel Taylor Coleridge stayed on their first tour through the Lake District in 1797.

Buried in the churchyard, not far from Wordsworth, is SIR JOHN RICHARDSON (1787–1865), a doctor and naturalist who settled in Lancrigg, just north of Grasmere, in 1855, after surviving two expeditions to the Arctic Circle with Sir John Franklin in search of the North West Passage in the 1820s, and a third, in 1847–9, to search for Franklin himself. His books on the fauna and wildlife of the Arctic are still considered essential reading.

Every summer, on or near St Oswald's Day (5 August), Grasmere stages a RUSHBEARING CEREMONY, when a procession of clergy and children carry a cross made of rushes through the village to the church. It is an ancient custom that celebrates the days when sweet-smelling rushes were used to cover the earthen floors of the local churches.

Rydal Water

Like a fair sister of the sky
Unruffled doth the blue lake lie
The mountains looking on
WILLIAM WORDSWORTH

RYDAL WATER is fed from Grasmere
by the River Rothay and was once
known as Rothaymere. It is one of
Lakeland's smallest lakes, just ¾ mile
(1.2 km) long, ¼ mile (400 m) wide
and up to 55 ft (17 m) deep. It is also
one of the most placid of the lakes,
and in the right conditions can create
a perfect mirror-image reflection of
the surrounding landscape.

In the hill above the lake, on the
southern shore, there is a huge cavern
known as RYDAL CAVE, the remnants
of former quarry workings.

Rydal Hall

Sixteenth-century RYDAL HALL at the
eastern end of the lake was for 400
years the home of the Le Flemings.
In 1963 it became a retreat for the
Diocese of Carlisle. The formal
gardens of the hall, which are being
restored, were designed by THOMAS
MAWSON, a leading landscape architect of the late 19th century (*see*
Windermere). There are waterfalls in
the park, and at the foot of one of
them is the FIRST KNOWN PURPOSE-
BUILT VIEWING HOUSE IN BRITAIN, put
there in 1669.

Rydal Church

In 1824 Lady Le Fleming had the
church of St Mary's built below Rydal
Mount, on a site chosen by
Wordsworth. The gallery inside was
reserved for the Le Flemings, while
the Wordsworths had two family pews
at the front. Wordsworth was church-
warden for a while in 1833–4.

At the western end of Rydal Water
is a small rock reached by some steps,
where Wordsworth used to sit and
look out over the lake. This was reput-
edly his favourite viewpoint and is
known as WORDSWORTH'S SEAT.

Nab Cottage

'Little Peggy Simpson was standing at the
door catching hailstones in her hand'
DOROTHY WORDSWORTH,
on walking past Nab Cottage in 1802

By the road that runs along the northern shore of Rydal Water, beneath the
towering Nab Scar, is NAB COTTAGE,
displaying the date 1702 over its front

door. Farmer's daughter 'LITTLE PEGGY SIMPSON' soon grew up and caught the eye of author THOMAS DE QUINCEY who was living up the road at Dove Cottage. He married her in 1816 and she became a loyal wife to him despite his debts and his opium habit (*see* page 14), and bore him eight children before her death in 1837.

In 1820 Peggy and de Quincey and their family moved to FOX GHYLL, down the river towards Ambleside, now a guest-house.

In 1838 Nab Cottage became the home of the poet HARTLEY COLERIDGE (1796–1849), eldest son of Samuel Taylor Coleridge. Like de Quincey, he wanted to be close to Wordsworth, who had become something of a father figure after Hartley's own father had walked out on his family at Greta Hall in 1803. Wordsworth was extremely fond of Hartley but had always feared for him, recognising him as a dreamy, unworldly character, partial to drink, who would struggle to make it through life.

Oh blessed vision! happy child!
Thou art so exquisitely wild,
I think of thee with many fears
For what may be thy lot in future years.

When Hartley died in 1849, aged 52, Wordsworth asked the vicar at Grasmere to keep the grave next to Hartley for him, and within a year the great man was lying next to his fellow poet.

Elterwater and the Langdale Valleys

Of Ancient Men and Smugglers

ELTERWATER IS THE SMALLEST OF THE 16 LAKES, ½ mile (800 m) long, ¼ mile (400 m) wide and 50 ft (15 m) deep. It lies at the heart of the Lake District where the two Langdale valleys converge beneath the twin peaks of Lakeland's most distinctive mountain-tops, the LANGDALE PIKES. It is fed by both Langdale Beck and the River Brathay, which then flows on eastwards, forming the boundary between the old county of Westmorland and the old Lancashire district of Furness, to meet Wordsworth Country at the head of Windermere, near Ambleside.

Great Langdale Valley

GREAT LANGDALE VALLEY IS THE OLDEST INHABITED PLACE IN THE LAKE DISTRICT, and is endowed with some impressive examples of prehistoric rock art dating from neolithic times. These can be found on what are known as the LANGDALE BOULDERS at COPT HOWE near Chapel Stile. Great Langdale is also one of the quieter valleys in the Lake District, and as such was popular in the 19th century with smugglers who would bring in spirits from the Isle of Man, where liquor was free of tax.

Near the head of the valley there is a relatively gentle if slightly twee pathway laid out by the National Trust that climbs up to STICKLE TARN, lying at 1,552 ft (473 m) in a dramatic location under the stern eastern face of Harrison Stickle. Nearby DUNGEON GHYLL, where a splendid waterfall plummets for 60 ft (18 m) down a precipitous ravine, is harder to find but worth the effort. The waterfall, DUNGEON GHYLL FORCE, inspired Wordsworth's poem 'The Idle Shepherd Boys'. (In the Lake District a waterfall is known as a 'force'.)

Little Langdale Valley

LITTLE LANGDALE VALLEY gathers in waters from the beauty spot of Blea Tarn and from the River Brathay, which rises near the Three Shires Stone at the top of Wrynose Pass and runs by Greenbank Farm before entering Little Langdale Tarn and then on to Little Langdale village and the Three Shires Inn.

Lanty Slee

GREENBANK FARM was the home of the Lake District's most notorious moonshiner, LANCELOT 'LANTY' SLEE, born in Borrowdale in 1800 of Irish descent. He farmed by day and operated illicit stills hidden in the fells around Langdale by night; and he frequently ended up in court in

Ambleside but was rarely convicted because the magistrates were his best customers. He died at Greenbank Farm at the age of 78, mourned by all, the secret locations of his stills dying with him.

Skelwith Force

After Little Langdale the River Brathay tumbles over the spectacular COLWITH FORCE and turns north to join Elterwater. Below the lake and above Skelwith Bridge, the river is squeezed through a deep rock channel to form the dramatic SKELWITH FORCE, only 15 ft (4.6 m) in height but mighty impressive after rain.

Ambleside

Lake District Icon

Although not geographically quite at the centre of the Lake District, AMBLESIDE is very much the region's spiritual centre. All roads lead to Ambleside and all visitors to Lakeland inevitably end up in Ambleside. It is the iconic Lakeland town, sturdy, grey-stone, picturesque and hearty, and boasts the LAKE DISTRICT'S MOST FAMOUS MAN-MADE LANDMARK, the quaint, miniature BRIDGE HOUSE, constructed above the Stock Beck to save on land tax. This dainty little structure was originally built in the early 18th century as an apple store for the Braithwaites of Old Ambleside Hall, and was at one time home to a family of eight. It was saved from ruination by local people and in 1946 became THE FIRST NATIONAL TRUST INFORMATION CENTRE, a function it still performs to this day.

Stock Beck once powered five mills, and is fed through the spectacular STOCK GHYLL FORCE, a 70 ft (21 m) waterfall that cascades down a mossy cleft behind the Salutation Hotel.

The Romans were quick to recognise the strategic importance of this location at the head of England's biggest lake, and established the fort of GALAVA there, with connections by road to their fort at Penrith and the port at Ravenglass. The Ambleside of today is a largely Victorian creation, built to accommodate the tourists brought here by the poetry of William Wordsworth and the steamboats of the Windermere Iron Steamboat Company.

Ambleside's most visible feature is the elegant broached spire of ST MARY'S CHURCH, 180 ft (55 m) high and almost unique in the Lake District, which is more used to tiny bellcotes or square towers. It was designed and built by George Gilbert Scott in 1854 and holds its own as a delicate foil to the majestic hills that ring the town.

St Mary's contains a chapel dedicated to William Wordsworth, who had an office in Ambleside when he served as Distributor for Stamps in Westmorland.

As at Grasmere there is a Rushbearing parade through the town in July every year, which ends with a service in St Mary's.

Harriet Martineau
(1802–76)

Where Coniston had John Ruskin, Victorian Ambleside had HARRIET MARTINEAU, regarded by many as THE FIRST FEMALE SOCIOLOGIST and THE FIRST FEMALE JOURNALIST.

Harriet was born in Norwich, the daughter of a Unitarian textile manufacturer, and became wealthy and much admired for writing books and articles on religion, politics and economics. She was also a courageous champion of education and the vote for women. While her Unitarian family supported her progressive views on women, they were alienated when, in 1851, she published a book called *Letters on the Laws of Man's Nature and Development*, which rejected religious belief and in many ways predicted Charles Darwin's Theory of Evolution – Charles Darwin and more particularly his older brother Erasmus were prominent amongst her admirers.

In 1845, suffering from poor health, Harriet moved to the revivifying climes of Ambleside and built herself a fine house behind the town's Methodist chapel, which she called THE KNOLL, and here she lived for the rest of her life. Inspired by the Lakeland scenery and invigorated by the bracing mountain air she embarked on her most productive years of writ-

ing, encouraged by a constant stream of distinguished visitors such as Coleridge and Wordsworth, each of whom would plant two trees in the garden, which is today abundant with firs and spruce.

The Knoll is now run as a holiday cottage.

Well, I never knew this
about
THE CENTRAL LAKES

In 1827 Wordsworth bought three miners' cottages on Rydal Water, and transformed them into a comfortable home for his son Willie to live in, calling it WHITE MOSS HOUSE. It was the only house Wordsworth ever actually bought, all his others being rented.

THOMAS DE QUINCEY (1785–1859), who took over Dove Cottage in Grasmere after Wordsworth, is best

remembered for his book CONFESSIONS OF AN ENGLISH OPIUM-EATER, published in 1821.

LITTLE LANGDALE is the 'little lowly vale' in Wordworth's dramatic poem 'The Excursion' where the hermit, Solitary, chooses to live alone.

FOX HOWE, on the river below Loughrigg at the western end of Rydal Water, was built by DR THOMAS ARNOLD, headmaster of Rugby School, as a summer home, in 1833. Arnold's 11-year-old son, the poet MATTHEW ARNOLD, met William Wordsworth for the first time in that same year, at Rydal Mount, a seminal event in the young boy's life. Arnold's own poetry and his outlook on life were greatly influenced by Wordsworth, and he went on to edit a selection of Wordsworth's poems in 1879.

Ambleside is the home of GAYNOR SPORTS, thought to be THE LARGEST INDEPENDENT PURVEYOR OF OUTDOOR EQUIPMENT IN BRITAIN.

HARRIET MARTINEAU was a great fan of Charles Dickens, despite her suspicion that he might have used her as the model for the interfering busybody in *Bleak House*, Mrs Jellyby.

Sculptor JOSEFINA DE VASCONCELLOS lived most of her life in the Lake District, originally in Little Langdale and latterly in Ambleside. For many years, before her death at the age of 100 in July 2005, she was THE WORLD'S OLDEST LIVING SCULPTOR. Her most famous pieces include Mary and Child in St Paul's Cathedral in London and Reconciliation in Coventry Cathedral, part of a series on the theme of reconciliation, which includes sculptures at the Berlin Wall and in Hiroshima. Some truly exquisite examples of her sculpture can be seen in the Lake District, such as The Vision of St Bega at St Bees Priory and The Family of Man in Kendal Parish Church.

The North-Western Lakes (River Derwent)

Borrowdale ✦ Derwentwater ✦ Keswick ✦ Bassenthwaite Lake

Keswick Moot Hall, built in 1813, has an unusual one-handed clock

River Derwent

'The fairest of all rivers . . .
beauteous stream . . .'
WILLIAM WORDSWORTH

The RIVER DERWENT rises on the slopes of Scafell Pike, flows down through BORROWDALE and into DERWENTWATER, past KESWICK, on through BASSENTHWAITE LAKE to Cockermouth, finally reaching the sea at Workington.

Borrowdale

'A pageant of beauty from end to end'
ALFRED WAINWRIGHT

BORROWDALE is regarded by many people as the loveliest of all English valleys, possessing some fine examples of the many scenic charms of Lakeland.

There are only two routes in or out of Borrowdale, both of them daunting. One way is across the HONISTER PASS, amongst the highest and steepest roads in the Lake District, with a gradient in some places of 1 in 4. At the top of the pass is the HONIS- TER SLATE MINE, started by monks from Furness Abbey some 500 years ago and now open for tours. The other way is via the JAWS OF BORROWDALE, where the River Derwent squeezes through a narrow gorge between high crags.

Seathwaite

SEATHWAITE village sits at the end of a narrow road, sheltering beneath the highest Lakeland fells, and serves as a good starting point for those who wish to climb England's highest mountain, SCAFELL PIKE. A little way up the mountain is picturesque STOCKLEY BRIDGE, a packhorse bridge which is frequently washed away, while on the slopes of Grey Knotts to the west can be seen the remnants of the BORROW- DALE GRAPHITE MINE.

In the mid 16th century, experienced miners brought in from Germany to find and extract lead, silver and copper heard tell of a black substance used by the local farmers to mark their sheep, which had been found on the fells near Seathwaite after a storm had uprooted some trees. The miners recognised it as graphite, and remarkably, given that the Borrowdale mine is THE ONLY GRAPHITE MINE BRITAIN HAS EVER HAD, it turned out that Borrowdale graphite was THE PUREST AND MOST RARE GRAPHITE IN THE WORLD.

The graphite was found to have a number of uses apart from marking sheep. It was used as a medicine when mixed with wine or ale, for rust proofing and for the coating of cannonball moulds. It was valuable stuff and guard-houses were erected at the entrance to the mine to prevent looting, although a thriving black market seems to have existed, based at the George Hotel in Keswick. BORROW- DALE GRAPHITE was most famously used to make CUMBERLAND PENCILS (*see* Keswick).

Castle Crag

CASTLE CRAG is a rugged height above the Jaws of Borrowdale, with commanding views of what Alfred Wainwright calls 'the loveliest square mile in the Lake District'. It is the perfect place for the ancient hill fort that gives the valley its name – Borrowdale comes from the Norse *borga dal*, meaning 'valley of the fort'. There is a memorial on the summit to the men of Borrowdale who died in the First World War. On the eastern flank of the hill is the cave used as a summer home by MILLICAN DALTON (1867–1947), THE CAVEMAN OF BORROWDALE, who gave up his life as an insurance clerk in London to live as a hermit in the Lake District, surrounded only by the glories of nature.

King's Howe

KING'S HOWE is a magnificent viewpoint on the side of Grange Fell, across the Jaws of Borrowdale from Castle Crag. It was so named by Princess Louise as a memorial to her brother King Edward VII. Down at the bottom of the fell is the BOWDER STONE, the LARGEST SINGLE BOULDER IN THE LAKE DISTRICT, a 2,000-ton rock balanced precariously on its edge. It used to terrify passers-by, who thought it would topple over and crush them, but in fact the stone is completely stable, and today there is a ladder up to the top from which there are splendid views down through the Jaws towards Derwentwater. The Bowder Stone is made of

a rock unlike any other rock in the Lake District and must have been left behind by a retreating glacier.

Derwentwater

Queen of Lakes

Known as the 'Queen of Lakes', DERWENTWATER is one of the larger lakes, but quite shallow, averaging 15 ft (4.6 m) in depth and only 75 ft (23 m) at its deepest. Scenically it is, in many people's opinion, the loveliest and most varied of the Lakes.

Friar's Crag

FRIAR'S CRAG is a low, wooded promontory on the eastern shore of Derwentwater. The view from here was described by Ruskin as 'ONE OF THE THREE MOST BEAUTIFUL SCENES IN EUROPE', and an early visit there may have helped to inspire his outlook on life. Canon Rawnsley placed a memorial on the point, engraved with Ruskin's own words: 'The first thing which I remember as an event in life was being taken by my nurse to the brow of Friar's Crag on Derwentwater.'

Friar's Crag appears in Arthur Ransome's *Swallows and Amazons* as the children's lookout spot, Darien.

St Herbert's Island

Friar's Crag is so called because it served as an embarkation point for friars visiting the cell of St Herbert, who brought Christianity to the Lakes in the 7th century and lived on Derwentwater's biggest island, now named ST HERBERT'S ISLAND. He was a close companion of St Cuthbert of Lindisfarne, and St Cuthbert is thought to have visited the island once a year to pray there with his friend. The two saints died on the same day, 20 March 687.

Beatrix Potter knew and loved St Herbert's Island – she made it Owl Island in *The Tale of Squirrel Nutkin.*

Derwent Island

Monks from Fountains Abbey probably embarked at Friar's Crag as well, in their case to go to DERWENT ISLAND, which they once owned.

Today Derwent Island belongs to the National Trust and is the only one of Derwentwater's four islands still inhabited. The island almost hides amongst its trees a house large enough to have upset William Wordsworth, who thought it spoiled the view. It was built in 1778 by an eccentric Nottinghamshire banker called JOSEPH POCKLINGTON, who wanted to jazz the area up a bit to attract tourists. In this good cause he built an obelisk and a druid's temple on the island, and instituted a regatta for which he would start races by firing a cannon from his new gun battery. He also built BARROW HOUSE (now a youth hostel) a little further south on the lake shore, where he diverted Barrow Brook to create a brand-new waterfall for the garden.

In 1844 DERWENT ISLAND HOUSE was given a new wing and a tower, designed by Anthony Salvin.

Lord's Island

Further south is LORD'S ISLAND, once the home of the EARL OF DERWENT-WATER, and at that time attached to the mainland by a drawbridge. The title was forfeit when the 3rd Earl lost his head for supporting the Jacobite Risings of 1715, and his grand house was demolished, the stones used to build the Moot Hall in Keswick.

The Road to Watendlath

Near the youth hostel at Barrow Hall on Derwentwater's eastern shore is a steep lane that leads up through woods towards the tiny National Trust village of WATENDLATH. About 400 yards (365 m) up this lane Barrow Brook chatters under a quaint pack-horse bridge called ASHNESS BRIDGE, which is perhaps THE MOST PHOTOGRAPHED BRIDGE IN THE LAKE DISTRICT – the view of Derwentwater from above the bridge is deservedly

an iconic Lakeland scene. Nearby there is a cairn in memory of BOB GRAHAM, who gives his name to the BOB GRAHAM ROUND. His actual grave is in the churchyard of St Andrew's in Stonethwaite.

A little further up the lane is SURPRISE VIEW, a superb vantage point across Derwentwater that can certainly take the unwary sightseer by surprise, being a precarious cliff edge hidden by trees until the last moment.

Watendlath

'Watendlath's quiet nook.
A farm is there, and a slated barn,
And a waterfall, and a pebbly tarn.'
EDMUND CASSON

WATENDLATH itself takes a long time to reach because the road is so narrow and winding, and it didn't even have a telephone line until 1984. The effort, however, is not wasted. The village only consists of a few cottages, a tea-

---

The Bob Graham Round

In 1932, Bob Graham, 42-year-old owner of a guest-house in Keswick, completed a 72-mile (116 km) circuit of 42 Lakeland peaks in 24 hours, a record that, unsurprisingly, remained unbroken for 28 years. Today, every summer, and even though the record has now been broken several times, people come from everywhere to try and emulate Bob Graham's achievement, and so win coveted membership of the prestigious BOB GRAHAM 24 HOUR CLUB.

room, and a farm with a herd of Herdwick sheep, but the setting beside Watendlath Tarn is ravishing, and the worthy subject of a painting by DORA CARRINGTON which hangs in Tate Britain.

Writer SIR HUGH WALPOLE (1884–1941) used Foldhead Farm at Watendlath as his setting for Rogue Herries Farm, the home of Judith Paris in his popular HERRIES CHRONICLE, a series of four novels about a Cumberland family, which introduced the Lakes to a huge new audience. Walpole lived in the Lake District for 17 years, in a house overlooking Derwentwater called BRACKENBURN, which appears in another Herries novel, *Vanessa.* He is buried in St John's churchyard in Keswick.

Lodore Falls

Watendlath Tarn feeds Watendlath Beck, which runs away under another very pretty packhorse bridge, and eventually cascades down nearly 100 ft (30 m) into the Borrowdale valley over the celebrated LODORE FALLS –

spectacular after rain. 'How does the water come down at Lodore?' asks the poet Robert Southey in a popular onomatopoeic poem – '. . . dashing and clashing and splashing,' he writes, answering his own question.

National Trust First

BRANDELHOW, 108 acres (43.7 ha) of woodland and pasture on the western shore of Derwentwater, was THE FIRST PROPERTY EVER PURCHASED BY THE NATIONAL TRUST. Queen Victoria's daughter PRINCESS LOUISE performed the opening ceremony on 6 October 1902, along with the three founders of the Trust, CANON HARDWICKE RAWNSLEY, OCTAVIA HILL and SIR ROBERT HUNTER, and each of them, including the Princess, planted an oak tree. The four trees, along with a commemorative stone, can be seen beside the road at Grid Reference 249204 (Ordnance Survey Landranger Map 89).

Mr McGregor's Garden

There are two large houses on the western shore of Derwentwater, LINGHOLM and FAWE PARK, that can only be glimpsed through trees from a nearby footpath, but are both nonetheless known throughout the world.

Lingholm is a mid-Victorian pile where Beatrix Potter and her parents spent many summer holidays between 1885 and 1905. Beatrix loved to explore the surrounding woods, which abound with red squirrels and other woodland creatures, and the sketches she made there became the background for *The Tale of Squirrel Nutkin*. Mr McGregor's famous garden in *The Tale of Peter Rabbit* and *The Tale of Benjamin Bunny* contains elements of the vegetable gardens at both Lingholm (with its wicket gate) and next-door Fawe Park, where the Potters stayed in 1903.

Fawe Park

The houses are private and not open to the public, but Lingholm's gardens are renowned for their azaleas and rhododendrons which, when in bloom, can be seen from the lake.

Newlands Valley

Peaceful NEWLANDS VALLEY to the west, which runs north to south parallel with Derwentwater, and is separated from the lake to the west by CATBELLS mountain, is the setting for Beatrix Potter's *The Tale of Mrs Tiggywinkle*. Real-life LUCIE CARR,

who was the daughter of the vicar of tiny whitewashed NEWLANDS CHURCH, is the star of the story, which opens with the line, 'Once upon a time there was a little girl called Lucie, who lived at a farm called Little-town.'

Other than the church, the most famous landmark in Newlands Valley used to be the remote RIGG BECK, a wooden Canadian-style property known as the Purple House because of its purple-painted clapboarding. Built in the 1880s as a hotel, it had more recently provided lodgings for actors appearing at the theatre in Keswick such as Tom Courtenay, Bob Hoskins, Victoria Wood and the poet Ted Hughes. Sadly, it was destroyed by fire in 2008.

Rigg Beck

From Elizabethan times until the end of the 19th century, Newlands Valley was extensively mined for lead, copper, silver and gold. The GOLD-SCOPE MINE at the southern end of the valley got its name from the German *Gottesgab*, meaning 'God's gift', because it was so productive in lead and copper.

The route out of Newlands Valley to the south is over the NEWLANDS PASS to Buttermere. A short path from the car park at the top of the pass leads to MOSS FORCE, a dramatic waterfall in three sections.

Keswick

Capital of the North Lakes

KESWICK lies like a gleaming jewel in a green bowl, with the grey bulk of Skiddaw to the north and blue Derwentwater to the south. Its name, Old English *cese wic*, means 'cheese farm', and in 1276 Edward I granted Keswick a charter for a market, selling not just cheese but all types of agricultural products from the surrounding farms.

In the mid 16th century minerals were discovered in the hills and Keswick became an important mining centre. Experienced miners were brought in from Germany to find and extract the lead, silver and copper, and remains of their encampments can be found all around Derwentwater, even on the islands.

Pencils

In the mid 16th century graphite was found near Seathwaite in Borrowdale. This graphite, or 'wadd' as it was called, turned out to be an excellent writing material, and a cottage industry grew up around Keswick for making THE WORLD'S FIRST GRAPHITE PENCILS, with one JOHN LADYMAN being acknowledged as THE FIRST KNOWN PENCIL-MAKER. Flemish traders took the pencils to Europe, where they became particularly popular with the students at the Italian art schools.

Early editions of the *Encyclopaedia Britannica* name a pencil factory belonging to a GEORGE ROWNEY as existing in Keswick in 1798, which would make it THE WORLD'S FIRST PENCIL FACTORY – but unfortunately the exact records have been lost and so that accolade officially goes to another Keswick factory which opened in 1832. This eventually became the CUMBER-LAND PENCIL COMPANY, which still

exists as THE WORLD'S OLDEST MANU-
FACTURER OF GRAPHITE PENCILS.

Q Section

During the Second World War
specially selected staff at the Cumberland Pencil Company, who were
sworn to secrecy, produced a number
of special green-painted pencils,
inside which were hidden a rolled-
up map of Germany and a compass.
The maps detailed escape routes out
of Germany and were given to
bomber aircrews and others sent
behind enemy lines, and were also
sent to prisoner-of-war camps. They
proved a vital lifeline to British
personnel who found themselves
trapped in Germany – as well as
giving the producers of the James
Bond films some ideas for Q's
gadgetry such as the exploding pen
in *From Russia with Love*.

The Borrowdale graphite
mine closed in 1890, but the
Cumberland Pencil Company
still make pencils in Keswick
today, producing 500,000
pencils every week, using low-
grade graphite mix imported
from all over the world.

Poet's Corner

In 1800 the poet SAMUEL
TAYLOR COLERIDGE (1772–
1834) came with his family to

live at the newly built GRETA HALL, up
on a hill behind the school in Keswick.
He was drawn there by the presence of
his friend William Wordsworth, who
was living in nearby Grasmere. 'I question if there be a room in England
which commands a view of mountains
and lakes and woods superior to that
in which I am now writing,' he noted
– words as true today as when he
penned them 200 years ago.

It is not for man to rest in
absolute contentment;
He is born to hopes and aspirations
as the sparks fly upward.

The writer of these words, the poet
ROBERT SOUTHEY (1774–1843), whose
wife was the sister of Coleridge's wife,
came to Greta Hall with his family
in 1803, and for a year the two families lived there together. Coleridge left
in 1804 when he had a breakdown
and became ill, but Southey stayed
there for 40 years, supporting both
families and declaring Greta Hall
'perhaps the finest single spot in
England'. In 1813 he was made Poet

Laureate by George III, on the recommendation of Sir Walter Scott. Southey's re-telling of a local tale was the origin of the popular children's story *Goldilocks and the Three Bears*. Coleridge, Southey and Wordsworth collectively became known as THE LAKE POETS.

Southey is buried in the churchyard of St Kentigern's at Great Crosthwaite, an old village on the outskirts of Keswick to the north. In 1909 Greta Hall was bought by Canon Hardwicke Rawnsley, the Vicar of Great Crosthwaite (*see* National Trust).

St Kentigern's, Crosthwaite

ST KENTIGERN'S, CROSTHWAITE, sits somewhat aloof on a little hill overlooking Keswick from the north, an ancient Christian site that existed long before Keswick. St Kentigern, also known as St Mungo, built a chapel here in AD 553 and there has been a church on the spot ever since. The present building, which contains some Norman work, dates mainly from 1523 and boasts a complete set of 16th-century consecration crosses, marking where the bishop sprinkled holy water on the day the church was consecrated. There are 12 outside and nine inside, forming THE ONLY COMPLETE SET OF CONSECRATION CROSSES IN ANY CHURCH IN ENGLAND. An enjoyable time can be spent looking for them all. In the church there is a

striking memorial to Southey with a long epitaph written by William Wordsworth.

Ye vales and hills whose
beauty hither drew
The poet's steps,
and fixed him here, on you,
His eyes have closed!

The huge churchyard contains the graves of a number of distinguished persons in addition to Robert Southey, amongst them CANON RAWNSLEY, founder of the National Trust, MAJOR-GENERAL SIR JOHN WOODFORD, wounded by the last shot fired at Corunna, and SIR EDMUND HENDERSON, founder of Scotland Yard's Criminal Investigation Department (CID).

Castlerigg

A short walk from Keswick, on top of a hill to the east, is CASTLERIGG STONE CIRCLE, which must be one of the most spectacularly sited ancient monuments anywhere. From within the circle it is possible to see most

of the Lake District's highest peaks, and the unchanging view still has the power to strike awe into the heart of modern man, just as it must have done when the circle was constructed over 5,000 years ago – Castlerigg is one of the earliest stone circles in Europe and was erected in 3200 BC. It is apparently impossible to count the number of stones – each attempt produces a different answer – although English Heritage, who run the site for the National Trust, give the official total as 40.

Bassenthwaite Lake

Farthest North

BASSENTHWAITE LAKE is THE MOST NORTHERLY LAKE IN THE LAKE DISTRICT, and THE ONLY LAKE TO BE ACTUALLY CALLED A LAKE – all the others being 'meres', 'waters' or 'tarns'. Some 4 miles (6.4 km) long and about ¾ mile (1.2 km) wide, it is the fourth largest of the lakes, but is actually quite shallow, just 70 ft (21 m) at its deepest point. Bassenthwaite Lake and Derwentwater are THE ONLY PLACES IN THE WORLD WHERE VENDACE ARE FOUND, vendace being a rare and endangered species of white fish.

St Bega's

... to a chapel nigh the field,
A broken chancel with a broken cross,
That stood on a dark
straight of barren land
ALFRED, LORD TENNYSON,
'Morte d'Arthur'

Sitting in lush green fields on the east bank of Bassenthwaite Lake, near the water's edge, is the small church of ST BEGA'S, encircled by a stone wall and dwarfed beneath the brown green bulk of Ullock Pike. There are only two other churches in the whole of England dedicated to St Bega, one at St Bees (*see* The Lakeland Coast) and one in Ennerdale, and it is likely that St Bega chose this beautiful and lonely spot for herself as a place to retire in her later years – there is certainly no other obvious reason for the church to be here. It is mighty difficult to find, lying at the end of a long grassy track, well away from any road and surrounded only by sheep.

The present building, which was restored in 1874, is mainly Norman, although there are signs of early Saxon work in the walls and two delightfully crooked arches inside that appear to be pre-Norman. The memorials are mainly to the Speddings, who for 300 years have lived at Mirehouse, a big grey mansion close by the church, which can be glimpsed through the trees.

Mirehouse

I heard the ripple washing in the reeds
And the wild water lapping on the crag
ALFRED, LORD TENNYSON, 'Morte d'Arthur'

MIREHOUSE was built by the Earl of Derby in 1666, and has been the home of the Spedding family since 1802. During the 19th century Mirehouse was something of an artistic powerhouse, as the family were friends with many of the creative giants of the age, such as Wordsworth, Tennyson, Southey, Thomas Carlyle and John Constable.

One literary owner was JAMES SPEDDING, born at Mirehouse in 1808. After a short career in the Colonial Office, he went with Lord Ashburton to America to negotiate the Webster–Ashburton Agreement of 1842, which established the north-eastern boundary between the US and Canada. He is best remembered, however, for his editing of the works of Francis Bacon, many of which are on display

at Mirehouse. He was described by his friend Alfred, Lord Tennyson, as 'the wisest man I know'.

Coleridge and Thackeray came to Mirehouse to stay with James, as did Alfred, Lord Tennyson, who wrote 'Morte d'Arthur' while staying there – he refers in the poem to St Bega's Church, which at that time was somewhat derelict (*see* page 26).

James Spedding died in 1881, eight days after being knocked down by a cab in London.

In 1974 a simple open-air theatre was built by the lake near the church, where on summer evenings 'Morte d'Arthur' is occasionally given a reading by members of the Tennyson Society. Tennyson used Bassenthwaite Lake as the inspiration for the scene where Sir Bedivere throws King Arthur's sword Excalibur into the lake.

Well, I never knew this *about*

THE NORTH-WESTERN LAKES (RIVER DERWENT)

SEATHWAITE is officially THE WETTEST INHABITED PLACE IN ENGLAND, with an average annual rainfall of between 130 and 140 inches (330 and 355 cm).

The German miners who came to Cumberland in the 16th century brought with them not just their mining skills but the recipe for that most delicious of culinary delights, the CUMBERLAND SAUSAGE.

Lead pencils do not actually contain lead but are so called because those who discovered the graphite in Borrowdale originally thought it was a kind of lead, which they called black lead. The illegal market in this black lead is thought to have been the origin of the phrase 'black market'.

The CUMBERLAND PENCIL MUSEUM in Keswick is home to THE LARGEST PENCIL IN THE WORLD.

BEATRIX POTTER used Cumberland pencils for writing and illustrating her books.

Next to the Pencil Museum is another of Keswick's unique attractions, the hugely enjoyable CARS OF THE STARS MUSEUM, which houses an impressive selection of cars from the film world, including many from the James Bond movies. There is the first Japanese sports car, the Toyota 2000 GT from *You Only Live Twice*, the red Mustang that performed on two wheels during the chase through Las Vegas in *Diamonds Are Forever*, the submarine Lotus Esprit from *The Spy Who Loved Me*, Bond's speedboat from the river chase in the opening scenes of *The World Is Not Enough*, and the invisible Aston Martin from *Die Another Day* – a bit hard to see but they assure us that it's there. The exhibits certainly leave you stirred, if not shaken. Another star is Del Boy's yellow Reliant Robin from TV's *Only Fools and Horses*.

FORCE CRAG MINE, 4 miles (6.4 km) west of Keswick at the head of the Coledale Valley, was THE LAST WORK-ING METAL MINE IN THE LAKE DISTRICT. It was finally abandoned in 1991. Now owned by the National Trust, the processing mill with its UNIQUE COLLECTION OF MINING MACHINERY is open to the public.

The WHINLATTER FOREST, west of Keswick, is THE ONLY MOUNTAIN FOREST IN ENGLAND and boasts THE LAKE DISTRICT'S LONGEST PURPOSE-BUILT MOUNTAIN BIKE TRAIL.

OVERWATER, north of Bassenthwaite, is the northernmost body of water in the Lake District.

The North-Western Lakes (River Cocker)

Buttermere ✦ Crummock Water ✦ Vale of Lorton ✦ Cockermouth

Wordsworth House, birthplace in 1770 of William Wordsworth

River Cocker

From Buttermere to Cockermouth

The RIVER COCKER rises in the fells above Buttermere, then flows through CRUMMOCK WATER and the VALE OF LORTON to meet the River Derwent at COCKERMOUTH. The name 'Cocker' comes from the Celtic word *kukra* meaning crooked.

Buttermere

Sons and Daughters

BUTTERMERE is as enchanting as its name, a small tranquil lake, not much over 1 mile (1.6 km) long, that is constantly changing colour as the sun breaks back and forth through the surrounding mountains. Owned by the National Trust, it was once joined to Crummock Water (and possibly

Loweswater) but the two bigger lakes are now divided by a rich greensward on which stands the hamlet of Buttermere, which takes its name from the lake and is not much more than a farm, a couple of houses and a hotel, all of them buzzing with activity in the summer months.

Perched on its own little crag above the scene is the small, plain church of St James. One of its windows

contains a plaque in memory of ALFRED WAINWRIGHT (1907–91), Lakeland's favourite son and most passionate advocate and guide (*see* Windermere), which urges the visitor to 'lift your eyes to Haystacks, his favourite place'. Wainwright's ashes are scattered on Haystacks.

The Beauty of Buttermere

MARY ROBINSON, daughter of the landlord of the Fish Hotel in Buttermere, was renowned for her beauty and grace, as trumpeted by Joseph Budworth in his *A Fortnight's Ramble to the Lakes*, one of the first-ever guide-

books. People came from far and wide to gaze upon this Lakeland treasure, including, in 1802, slick, handsome, nattily dressed the Hon. Augustus Hope, who asked for her hand in marriage. Although he was 25 years older than Mary, she accepted his offer with much joy (and with her father's eager blessing), for Hope was apparently a wealthy and honourable man, brother of the Earl of Hopetoun and an MP to boot.

They were married in Lorton Church just down the road, and all might have been well had not the blabbermouth Samuel Taylor Coleridge written about the wedding in a London paper, with the result that Hope was recognised as an impostor by a friend of the real Augustus Hope. It turned out that the bridegroom's actual name was JOHN HATFIELD, and he already had a wife and children, and had spent a considerable time in prison for forgery and fraud. Hatfield fled to Wales but was apprehended in Swansea, then tried and hanged in Carlisle, and poor Mary was left alone at the inn, nursing her heartbreak. Her sad tale was mentioned in the romantic verse of William Wordsworth's 'The Prelude'.

All was not entirely lost, however. As a result of all the publicity, business boomed at the Fish Hotel, and Mary eventually married a good man and true from Caldbeck, and together they took over the hotel when her parents retired. Mary is buried in the churchyard at Caldbeck, not far from John Peel (*see* Caldbeck).

Crummock Water

Fed by Force

CRUMMOCK WATER is one of the lesser-known lakes, but no less beauteous for that. It is 2½ miles (4 km) long and quite deep – 144 ft (44 m) in some places. It is fed by the River Cocker from Buttermere, by the waters that tumble over the celebrated Scale Force, and by a stream from Loweswater.

Powered boats are banned here, which keeps the lake peaceful, although little RANNERDALE to the east was far from quiet in the 11th century when the invading Normans had a disagreeable confrontation there with a number of the locals under Earl Beothar. Apparently, it is thanks to so much blood being spilt on that occasion that the valley produces an especially rich pageant of bluebells in the spring.

Scale Force

'Scale Force, the white downfall of
which glimmered through the trees,
that hang before it like the bushy
hair over a madman's eyes'
SAMUEL TAYLOR COLERIDGE

One of the Lakes' more hidden treasures, SCALE FORCE tumbles down the northern flank of Red Pike above Crummock Water, and can only be reached from Buttermere by a walk of about an hour. The route begins in water meadows, crosses over an old humpbacked bridge, and then follows along a gently rising stone path, which though undemanding at first becomes quite rocky, steep and slippery towards the end.

The waterfall when you get there is quite lovely, a delicate strand of white lace threading its way down a deep, wooded gully, splayed out at the bottom into a wide skirt of bubbling water. It is THE HIGHEST WATERFALL IN THE LAKE DISTRICT, with a total drop of 170 ft (52 m), made up of one single drop of 120 ft (37 m) and a number of smaller drops.

Loweswater

LOWESWATER is one of the smaller lakes, 1 mile (1.6 km) long, ½ mile (800 m) wide and about 60 ft (18 m) deep. There is a good footpath that goes all the way round, and the heavily wooded southern shore abounds with red squirrels. Rowing boats can be hired from the National Trust for exploring the lake itself.

Vale of Lorton

There is a Yew-tree, pride of Lorton Vale,
Which to this day stands single,
in the midst
Of its own darkness, as it stood of yore.
WILLIAM WORDSWORTH

The village hall in LORTON, situated between Crummock Water and Cockermouth, is called the YEW TREE HALL in honour of the noble, if slightly battered, old yew that stands on the opposite side of the Whit Beck. Both George Fox, the founder of the Quaker movement, and John Wesley,

the founder of the Methodists, stood beneath this ancient tree to preach to vast crowds, and Wordsworth was so impressed he wrote a poem about it, called Yew Trees.

Yew Tree Hall is the site of the original Jennings Brewery (*see* Cockermouth). The Jennings family began brewing ale on their family farm, High Swinside, in the early 19th century, most of it going to the old Horseshoe Inn in Lorton. The ale proved so popular that they had to build a proper brewery on the Whit Beck, and when that proved too small Jennings moved to Cockermouth and the Lorton brewery became the village hall.

Lorton stands at the western end of the WHINLATTER PASS, which climbs to a height of 1,043 ft (318 m) on its way to Keswick.

Cockermouth

Pure Waters

COCKERMOUTH is a delightfully colourful place of Georgian streets, pretty cobbled alleyways and narrow lanes that wind down to the riverside. The town grew up beside a Norman castle on a hill, built to guard the lowest crossing point on the fast-flowing River Derwent, at its confluence with the River Cocker. The present castle, which dates from the 14th century, has been partially restored as a private home, but

much of it remains in a decorously ruinous state. The curtain wall and its watch-towers lean precariously over CUMBERLAND'S LAST REMAINING BREWERY, JENNINGS BREWERY, built at the foot of the hill to take advantage of the pure water from the castle well.

Mutiny, Poetry and the Stars

The churchyard in Cockermouth contains the graves of two proud fathers, John Wordsworth, father of William, and a hand-loom weaver named John Fallows whose son, Fearon Fallows, became the first astronomer at the Cape of Good Hope in South Africa.

Both these famous sons of Cockermouth went to school in the town, along with a slightly more controversial fellow, the mutineer Fletcher Christian.

Fletcher Christian
(1764–93)

FLETCHER CHRISTIAN was born at MOORLAND CLOSE, the family farm-house on the southern outskirts of Cockermouth. At 18 he joined the Royal Navy and in 1787 sailed with Captain Bligh to the West Indies as a midshipman. Christian impressed Bligh with his enthusiasm and leadership qualities, and in 1788 was chosen by Bligh to be first mate on HMS *Bounty* for a voyage to Tahiti to collect breadfruit samples to take to the plantation slaves on Jamaica. When they arrived in Tahiti after ten months at sea, the *Bounty*'s crew revelled in the sunshine and beauty of the island, and were equally beguiled by the warmth and friendliness of the Tahitian women. Christian fell in love with a girl called Maimiti and later married her.

Three weeks after leaving what they must have thought was heaven, the crew of the *Bounty*, led by Fletcher Christian, mutinied, cast Captain Bligh adrift in a small boat, and sailed back to Tahiti. The blame for the mutiny has often been attributed to Bligh's cruelty, but it seems just as likely that the sailors were reluctant to give up the idyllic lifestyle and womanly charms they had enjoyed on Tahiti to return to their harsh, cold, impoverished life in England.

Christian, with eight others and their womenfolk, searched the Pacific Ocean for an island where they could live safe from the vengeance of the Royal Navy. On 23 January 1790 they found PITCAIRN, a volcanic island 1,350 miles (2,170 km) south-east of Tahiti, named after Robert Pitcairn, the midshipman who had first sighted it in 1767. They landed, set fire to the *Bounty*, and settled down to a life in paradise. Unfortunately for them, life in paradise turned out to be pretty savage, and within 15 years all but one of the original mutineers, a chap called John Adam, were dead. Fletcher Christian left a son, THURSDAY OCTO-BER CHRISTIAN, THE FIRST CHILD BORN ON PITCAIRN ISLAND.

In 1838 the islanders were granted an amnesty and Pitcairn Island became a British colony. It is now THE LAST REMAINING BRITISH OVER-SEAS TERRITORY IN THE PACIFIC. Of the 50 or so inhabitants, almost all of them are direct descendants of the mutineers, many of them bearing the surname Christian. 'Tis a long way from Cockermouth.

William Wordsworth
(1770–1850)

Was it for this,
That one, the fairest of all rivers, loved
To blend his murmurs
with my nurse's song,

And from his alder shade and rocky falls,
And from his fords and
shallows sent a voice
That flowed along my dreams?
WILLIAM WORDSWORTH,
'The Prelude'

WILLIAM WORDSWORTH was born in 1770 in a splendidly handsome, many-windowed Georgian house at the end of tree-lined Main Street in Cocker-mouth, as was his sister Dorothy the following year. The house had been built not long before in 1745, and became the Wordsworth home in 1766 when the poet's father John was made steward to the owner Sir James Lowther. The River Derwent flows at the bottom of the garden and William, in his poem 'The Prelude', which he began at the age of 28, asks if the gentle murmurings of this fairest river awakened his desire to become a poet.

The property today is owned by the National Trust. The original stair-case, panelling and fireplaces are still in situ, and the house has been fitted throughout with 18th-century furni-ture to show how it must have been in Wordsworth's day. The garden is planted with flowers, trees and vegetables of the period.

Hanging on the wall of one of the rooms in what is now called Wordsworth House are two paintings of John and Rebecca Fallows, a weaver and his wife who lived in a tiny cottage just across the road. In July 1789, Rebecca gave birth in that cottage to another of Cockermouth's talented sons, Fearon Fallows.

Fearon Fallows
(1789–1831)

FEARON FALLOWS won a scholarship to Cambridge, where he studied mathematics, and in 1820 he was appointed to the position of FIRST ASTRONOMER TO GEORGE IV AT THE CAPE OF GOOD HOPE in South Africa, charged with overseeing the establishment of THE FIRST-EVER OBSERVATORY IN THE SOUTHERN HEMISPHERE. He died in South Africa of scarlet fever at the young age of 43, having catalogued over 300 stars of the southern skies.

Fallows was not the first mathematical genius to emerge from the environs of Cockermouth.

John Dalton
(1766–1844)

Over the door of a plain white weaver's cottage beside a narrow lane in the village of EAGLESFIELD, 2 miles (3.2 km) from Cockermouth, is a rough but proud inscription telling the world that this was the birthplace of JOHN DALTON, an Englishman who would grow up to have a profound influence on the development of the modern world. The son of a poor Quaker weaver, John Dalton was quickly recognised as a special talent, and by the tender age of 12 he was giving lessons to the younger children of the village in a local barn. It was during this time that he began to realise that he saw the world differently from the other children – for instance, the scarlet colour of a soldier's uniform and the green of grass both appeared to him as a shade of yellow, and what others called red he merely saw as a 'shade or defect of light'. His investigations into this phenomenon led him to be the FIRST PERSON TO RECOGNISE COLOUR-BLINDNESS.

Dalton went on to become Professor of Mathematics at Manchester University, where he was able to carry out copious experiments on chemicals, with which he ascertained that matter consisted of tiny particles or 'atoms'. This led to the publication in 1803 of his startling and groundbreaking THEORY OF ATOMIC WEIGHTS, which became THE BLUE-PRINT FOR CHEMICAL AND ATOMIC THEORY AND STUDY for the next 150 years.

Well, I never knew this *about*

THE NORTH-WESTERN LAKES (RIVER COCKER)

Like Cocker CRUMMOCK comes from 'crooked' in Celtic, and indeed Crummock Water does possess a kink, but the name probably refers to the whole valley.

The waters of LOWESWATER run east to feed Crummock Water, making Loweswater THE ONLY ONE OF THE LAKES TO DRAIN TOWARDS THE CENTRE OF THE LAKE DISTRICT.

In May 1568 Scottish royalty, in the shape of MARY QUEEN OF SCOTS, spent some precious hours of freedom in Cockermouth, at the Old Hall off the market-place, after fleeing from Scotland and landing on the Cumberland coast. Mary spent her first three nights in England, and her last three nights of freedom, in WORKINGTON HALL (now a ruin), where she was the guest of Sir Henry Curwen.

American royalty, in the shape of BING CROSBY, also enjoyed the hospitality of Cockermouth. He came for the salmon fishing on the River Derwent, and there is a faded picture of him in the bar of the TROUT HOTEL on Main Street.

The bronze bust of William Wordsworth that stands opposite Wordsworth House was unveiled on 7 April 1970 by William's great-great-grandson, to celebrate the bi-centenary of the poet's birth. As part of the same celebrations, 27,000 daffodils were planted around Cockermouth.

The impressive statue in Main Street, Cockermouth, is of the 6TH EARL OF MAYO, who was the town's MP from 1857 to 1868. He later became Viceroy of India and was assassinated while visiting the Andaman Islands in 1872.

In 2009 the RIVER COCKER broke its banks and flooded the centre of Cock-ermouth, causing immense damage. Further downstream, the RIVER DERWENT washed away three bridges in Workington, cutting the town in half.

For over 100 years, the now lost Quaker Meeting House at PARDSHAW, built in 1672, held THE LARGEST COUNTRY MEETING OF QUAKERS IN ENGLAND.

DOVENBY HALL, built around a 12th-century pele tower 2 miles (3.2 km) north of Cockermouth, is now the headquarters of the FORD WORLD RALLY TEAM.

THE LAKELAND COAST

WHITEHAVEN ✦ ST BEES ✦ CALDER

St Bees Priory dates from the 12th century and
boasts the finest Norman doorway in the North West

Whitehaven

Georgian Planning

At the end of the 16th century WHITE-
HAVEN was a miniscule fishing village
of nine thatched cottages. By the end
of the 17th century it had become
ENGLAND'S FIRST PLANNED TOWN
since the Middle Ages, with a population of 3,000, and was THE SECOND
LARGEST PORT ON THE WEST COAST OF
ENGLAND after Bristol. Behind this

growth were the LOWTHER FAMILY,
later EARLS OF LONSDALE, who developed Whitehaven as a port for

shipbuilding and the export of Cumberland coal.

The planning of the new town was inspired by what Christopher Wren was doing in London after the Great Fire of 1666, and Whitehaven's elegant grid pattern layout was even used as a template for the expansion of New York in America.

St James's Church

Whitehaven has over 250 listed buildings, most of them Georgian, one of the finest being ST JAMES'S CHURCH, which stands at the top of a hill overlooking the town and possesses what Pevsner described as 'THE FINEST GEORGIAN CHURCH INTERIOR IN THE COUNTY' (Cumberland).

It was built in 1753 to a design by CARLISLE SPEDDING (*see* below), and the galleried interior is sumptuous. Behind the altar is a remarkable paint-ing of the TRANSFIGURATION by GIULIO CESARE PROCACCINI, thought to have been removed from the Esco-rial Palace in Madrid by French soldiers during the Napoleonic Wars. It found its way into the possession of the 3rd Earl of Lonsdale, who gave it to the church in 1869, and it is THE ONLY WORK OF GIULIO CESARE PROCACCINI TO BE FOUND IN ANY ENGLISH CHURCH. The font, it is claimed, is from the DUOMO CATHE-DRAL IN FLORENCE.

American Connections

MILDRED GALE, paternal grand-mother of George Washington, first President of the United States, is buried somewhere in the churchyard of the ruined St Nicholas Church in the middle of Whitehaven, destroyed by fire in 1971. After the death of her first husband Lawrence Washington, by whom she had three children, including Augustine, father of George, she married a sea merchant called George Gale who had interests on both sides of the Atlantic. They settled in his home town of White-haven, where she died in 1701.

In 1778, during the American War of Independence, the American priva-teer JOHN PAUL JONES, born in Scot-land and apprenticed in Whitehaven, attacked

St Nicholas Church

the port in an attempt to destroy the fleet of coal ships at anchor. Despite having led a party ashore to spike the harbour's defensive guns, Jones was betrayed by one of his crew who warned the town, and little damage was done. There is a memorial to the event on the harbour front.

In 1782, in order to escape the war in America, English shipping agent DANIEL BROCKLEBANK transferred his BROCKLEBANK SHIPPING LINE, one of THE WORLD'S FIRST DEEP-SEA SHIPPING COMPANIES, from Massachusetts to Whitehaven. The company later moved on to Liverpool and eventually merged to become Cunard.

Whitehaven Mining

High above the old harbour at Whitehaven towers the CANDLESTICK CHIMNEY, built as an air shaft for one of Whitehaven's many coal-mines. The candlestick design was the suggestion of the mine's owner Lord Lonsdale, who when asked over dinner by his architect if he had any particular design in mind for the chimney, gestured to the candlesticks on his dining table and said, 'Build it like that!'

Carlisle Spedding
(1695–1755)

In 1729 CARLISLE SPEDDING, agent to the Lowther family, sank a coal-pit at SALTOM BAY, just to the south of Whitehaven, which was THE FIRST UNDERSEA COAL-MINE IN THE WORLD, reaching a depth of 456 ft (139 m). Spedding was something of a pioneer and was among THE FIRST TO USE STEAM ENGINES IN HIS MINES.

The Whitehaven pits were described as 'the most dangerous pits in all the world' because of the huge build-up of gases that regularly occurred inside. To try and counter the danger of explosions caused by the use of naked flames for illumination, Spedding invented THE FIRST 'SAFETY LAMP', a combination of brass and steel wheels, turned by a handle, in which a flint was struck to produce

sparks. It was known as the SPED-DING WHEEL. Although still highly dangerous, it was at least less lethal than a naked flame.

The Saltom Pit operated until 1848, and the ruins of the mine's surface workings and buildings have been preserved as a scheduled ancient monument.

William Brownrigg
(1711–1800)

Helping Spedding in his efforts to improve mining conditions was DR WILLIAM BROWNRIGG, who had a practice in Whitehaven at No. 24 Queen Street and was married to Spedding's niece Mary. As well as being a doctor, Brownrigg was a scientist, and he set up a laboratory close to one of the Lowther Mines, to which Spedding had gases from the mine piped over for Brownrigg to study. Brownrigg was THE FIRST PERSON TO SPOT THAT AN EXPLOSION WAS PRECEDED BY A FALL IN PRESSURE, and was thus able to make rough predictions of explosions in time to give some warning. Brownrigg's study of gases led to him being made a life member of the Royal Society.

Brownrigg also made a study of ways of making salt, in order to improve the quality, and he DISCOVERED PLATINUM, from a sample of a new material brought back from Jamaica by his brother-in-law Charles Wood.

BENJAMIN FRANKLIN asked to see Brownrigg while on a tour of Britain and Brownrigg took Franklin down one of the Whitehaven mines. On another occasion, while Franklin was visiting Brownrigg's home, Ormathwaite Hall near Keswick, the two went out in a boat on Derwentwater so that Franklin could demonstrate his party trick of 'pouring oil on troubled waters', by calming the choppy waters of the lake with olive oil.

St Bees

An Irish Princess and a Very Old Man

Legend has it that in the 9th or 10th century an Irish princess called BEGA, fleeing Ireland and a forced marriage to a Viking prince, was shipwrecked on the Cumberland coast and appealed to the local landowner Lord Egremont for land on which to build a nunnery. Canny chap that he was, milord told St Bega that she could have as much land as was covered by snow the next day – which just happened to be Midsummer's Day. Imagine his dismay when he woke up the following morning to find a large tract of land between his castle and the sea deep in snow. Most unfair.

The priory that stands at ST BEES today was founded as a Benedictine House in 1120, and was much restored

in the 19th century by WILLIAM BUTTERFIELD. Some good Norman pillars survive, and the west doorway is perhaps THE BEST NORMAN DOORWAY IN CUMBERLAND. There are two other, more modern treasures inside, an art nouveau metalwork screen by Butterfield, which separates the nave from the chancel, and in the Lady Chapel the sublime ST BEGA'S VISION, statues of St Bega and the Virgin Mary by the Lake District sculptor JOSEFINA DE VASCONCELLOS.

Outside, forming the lintel of an

alcove set in the wall between the west door and the vicarage, is the carved BEOWULF STONE, thought possibly to have come from the original nunnery, which shows an armoured figure killing a snarling dragon.

St Bees Man

In 1981, during an archeological dig in the south side of the chancel, a lead coffin was discovered. Inside was the body of a man of about 40, wrapped in a linen shroud impregnated with a resinous substance that had preserved the corpse remarkably well, to the extent that the anatomical structures of organs such as the heart, liver and kidneys were completely intact, and liquid blood was found in the chest cavity. ST BEES MAN, thought to have lived some time between 1300 and 1500, is THE BEST-PRESERVED MEDIEVAL BODY EVER FOUND IN ENGLAND.

St Bees School

Across the road from the priory is ST BEES SCHOOL, founded in 1583 by EDMUND GRINDAL, born at Cross Hill House in St Bees, the son of a local farmer, who became Archbishop of Canterbury under Elizabeth I. Old boys include:

THE REVD WILLIAM GILPIN (1724–1804), creator of the romantic ideal of the 'picturesque'. In his Observa-

tions of the River Wye, published in 1782, he urges the traveller to 'examine the face of a country by the rules of picturesque beauty'.

EDWARD CHRISTIAN, lawyer and brother of Fletcher Christian the mutineer (*see* Cockermouth).

CAPTAIN WILLIAM LEEFE ROBINSON (1895–1918) of the Royal Flying Corps, who won a Victoria Cross for being the first to shoot down an airship over Britain, in 1916.

ROWAN ATKINSON, TV comic actor and writer, creator of Mr Bean.

Calder Abbey

Old and New

The gnarled pink sandstone ruins of CALDER ABBEY hide away behind trees in a lost valley, where the only sounds are those of the wind and the birds and the fluttering of butterfly wings. It is so silent here that you can almost hear the trailing vegetation creeping amongst the stones, and the scrabbling of tiny beasts eating away at the foundations. Concealed from the road, and only barely glimpsed from the rough footpath running by, these must be among the least known and most romantic ruins in the country, and they are magical.

Great arches march in tangled desolation toward a squat, eyeless tower rising 60 ft (18 m) into the sky, and in the great vault beneath, open to the sky, rest three knights returned from the Crusades, lying beneath crumbling, ivy-covered stone tombs.

Attached to all this splendour, and no doubt plundered from it, is a remarkable brown house of the 18th century, later made grand in the style of the Arts and Crafts Movement, but

with an eerie, empty feel to it which only adds to the intriguing frisson of the place.

Calder Abbey was founded in 1134 by monks from Furness Abbey, but almost before they could settle there the place was raided by the Scots, and the monks were driven away – eventually, after many adventures, to found a new abbey at Byland in Yorkshire. In 1148 a new Cistercian House was formed at Calder, which flourished in a quiet way until the Dissolution of the Monasteries in 1536, when the estate was given to Henry VIII's principal agent in the north, the voracious Sir Thomas Leigh, who stripped the abbey buildings and reduced them to a shell.

In the 18th century the Senhouse family built ABBEY HOUSE on to the ruins, incorporating stone from the abbey, and this was expanded at the beginning of the 20th century to what we see there today. Rumour has it that there is a secret passage running beneath the house and leading to one of the original cells in the abbey . . .

Calder Abbey is a gem, hidden in a ravishing green valley, timeless and mysterious. But what makes it even more extraordinary is a sudden glimpse above the trees of a tall and sinister tower from a very different world, a shocking reminder of what lurks but 2 miles (3.2 km) away down the pretty, bubbling river.

Calder Hall

In the early 1950s CALDER HALL, situated where the River Calder meets the sea, became the site of THE WORLD'S FIRST COMMERCIAL NUCLEAR POWER STATION, and the site of BRITAIN'S FIRST PLUTONIUM-PRODUCING REACTORS (WINDSCALE). In 1957 Windscale almost became the site of THE WORLD'S FIRST LARGE-SCALE ATOMIC ACCIDENT, when one of the reactors overheated and caught fire, and the peace of the Calder Valley was shattered by convoys of buses evacuating panicked staff. Thanks, however, to the courage and quick thinking of the rescue team at Windscale, disaster was avoided, important lessons were learned, and the Calder Valley was able to sink back into the slumber of ages.

The whole nuclear complex is now known as SELLAFIELD, and the Calder Hall power station ceased operating in 2003. Sellafield is today home to Britain's nuclear reprocessing facilities, and includes a very smart visitor centre.

Well, I never knew this
about
THE LAKELAND COAST

The author JONATHAN SWIFT spent the first four years of his life in WHITE-HAVEN, kidnapped from Dublin by his devoted nanny, who couldn't bear to leave her young charge behind when she had to return home to White-haven to bid farewell to a dying relative. When Swift's mother discov-ered what had happened, she instructed the nanny to keep young Jonathan safe until he was old enough to make the trip back to Ireland alone. Swift loved his time in Whitehaven, where he lived in BOWLING GREEN HOUSE, perched high on the cliffs above the beach. Watching the tiny figures scurrying around on the sands below is said to have given him the idea for a race of very small people, who later appeared as the Lilliputians in his novel *Gulliver's Travels*. Bowl-ing Green House is still there, but private.

June 1998 saw the closure of JEFFER-SON WINE MERCHANTS in White-haven, THE OLDEST FAMILY WINE MERCHANT IN ENGLAND, which had traded from the same shop in Lowther Street for over two centuries. In May 2000, RUM STORY, THE WORLD'S FIRST EXHIBITION ABOUT RUM, opened in the premises.

Rum Story

ST BEES HEAD IS THE MOST WESTERLY POINT OF NORTHERN ENGLAND, and THE ONLY MAJOR SEA CLIFF BETWEEN WALES AND SCOTLAND. It is also the start of Alfred Wainwright's Coast to Coast walk.

St Bees gave Elizabeth I two arch-bishops, EDMUND GRINDAL, born in St Bees, who became Archbishop of Canterbury in 1575, and his child-hood friend EDWIN SANDYS, who grew up in St Bees and became Arch-bishop of York in 1576.

On the headland of St Bees there is a nature reserve run by the Royal Society for the Protection of Birds,

that is home to THE ONLY COLONY OF
BLACK GUILLEMOTS IN ENGLAND.

Towards the head of the Calder
valley, in a lonely spot on Cold Fell,
is the bewitching MONK'S BRIDGE,

its pink brick covered in moss. It
was used by the monks of Calder
Abbey to cross the deep chasm
of Friar Gill, and is THE OLDEST
PACKHORSE BRIDGE IN THE LAKE
DISTRICT.

THE WESTERN LAKES

ENNERDALE WATER ✦ WASDALE ✦
ESKDALE ✦ DUDDON VALLEY

Muncaster Castle, home of the Penningtons for over 800 years

Ennerdale Water

Furthest West

ENNERDALE WATER IS THE MOST WEST-
ERLY OF THE LAKES, and the most
remote, since it is the only lake without a road running beside it. It is 2½
miles (4 km) long, ¾ mile (1.2 km)
wide and up to 148 ft (45 m) deep.
The water is crystal clear and serves
as a reservoir for the towns of West
Cumberland. At the western end the
scenery is flat and looks across the
plains to the sea. Towards the eastern
end the scenery is mountainous, and
a 3-mile (5 km) walk east along the

valley of the River Liza brings you to
Pillar mountain, 2,927 ft (892 m) high,
with on its northern flank the distinctive PILLAR ROCK, known as THE
BIRTHPLACE OF ROCK CLIMBING, the
site in 1826 of THE FIRST RECORDED
ROCK CLIMB IN THE LAKE DISTRICT,
by John Atkinson of Ennerdale.

You see yon precipice, it almost looks
Like some vast building
made of many crags
And in the midst is one particular rock
That rises like a column from the vale,
Whence by our Shepherds it is
call'd, the Pillar.
WILLIAM WORDSWORTH

Ennerdale Water is the source of the RIVER EHEN, which was once used to cool the Sellafield nuclear power station. The River Ehen is THE ONLY RIVER IN ENGLAND WHERE THE RARE FRESHWATER PEARL MUSSEL IS THOUGHT TO BREED, and the river is also an important breeding ground for Atlantic salmon.

Wasdale

Deepest, Highest, Smallest, Biggest, Highest

WASDALE is the Lake District's Wild West, tucked away in a remote corner and blessed with some of Lakeland's most superlative scenery. The dale claims the deepest lake, the highest mountain, the smallest church, the biggest liar and the highest cross.

Wastwater

WASTWATER is ENGLAND'S DEEPEST LAKE, 258 ft (79 m) deep, 3 miles (5 km) long, nearly ½ mile (800 m) wide,

and overshadowed by dark, menacing cliffs called THE SCREES, which run the entire length of the south-east shore. Scree is made up of millions of broken rock fragments, and these precipitous scree slopes rise virtually sheer out of the lake to a height of almost 2,000 ft (610 m), at the summits of Illgill Head and Whin Rigg.

In tranquil weather the surface of Wastwater looks as smooth as glass, but when the scree slides and the rocks tumble into the lake, the black water boils and seethes like a living thing. In windy conditions spray can be felt hundreds of feet up on the mountainsides.

The view north-east along Wastwater towards Wasdale Head, showing YEWBARROW FELL, GREAT GABLE and LINGMELL FELL, has been used since 1951 as the Lake District logo, and has been voted BRITAIN'S FAVOURITE VIEW. It is indeed a magnificent and unforgettable view, this majestic array of England's high peaks.

Wasdale Head

WASDALE HEAD is a straggling collection of whitewashed buildings and dry-stone walls scattered about wide, pale green fields ringed with mountains.

It has a feel of America's Wild West, and it would come as no surprise to see cowboys galloping across the plain, although sheep are more likely. It is a dead end and can only be reached by a narrow, undulating road that winds its way between hillocks and crags along the northern edge of Wastwater. There is, even at the height of summer, a sense of being apart.

St Olaf's Church

Standing alone in a clump of yew trees is ST OLAF'S CHURCH, a long, low building with a tiny bellcote, a roof of enormous slate tiles and a fair claim to being THE SMALLEST CHURCH IN ENGLAND. The present building dates from 1550, but there are roof beams inside said to come from a Viking longship, indicating that this has been a place of worship for at least 1,000 years. In fact, being inside St Olaf's is a bit like being in an upturned boat: a clutter of wood, V-shaped roof of ancient wood beams, wooden pews and sloping walls, the whole seeming to gently rock. It is a soothing place.

Etched on to one of the diamond windowpanes is a picture of NAPES NEEDLE, a dramatic exposed rock pillar, 65 ft (20 m) high, on the flank of Great Gable. Below are the words 'I will lift up mine eyes unto the hills from whence cometh my strength', put there in memory of the members of the Fell and Rock Climbing Club who gave their lives in the First World War.

Along the windowsills are brass memorial plaques to climbers who have perished in the mountains, not just in the Lake District, but all over the world, for Wasdale Head is regarded as THE BIRTHPLACE OF ROCK CLIMBING everywhere.

The churchyard likewise contains the graves of some of those who died on the surrounding fells – for some reason the majority seem to have met their end on Great Gable.

Birthplace of British Rock Climbing

Wasdale Head is popular with rock climbers because it is surrounded by a huge variety of climbing challenges from 'very difficult' to 'extreme'. To the west is PILLAR ROCK, climbed in 1913 by Everest hero GEORGE MALLORY, who found a way up now called 'Mallory's Route'. To the east is ENGLAND'S BIGGEST CLIMBING CRAG, SCAFELL CRAG, and to the north is the famous, and deadly, NAPES NEEDLE.

In 1886 W.P. HASKETT SMITH

(1859–1946), THE FATHER OF ROCK CLIMBING, made a solo ascent of NAPES NEEDLE on Great Gable, leaving his handkerchief fluttering on the top to mark THE WORLD'S FIRST OFFICIAL SPORTING ROCK CLIMB. He stayed at the WASTWATER HOTEL, now the WASDALE HEAD INN, the first of the many thousands of rock climbers, amateur and professional, who have come to Wasdale and set out from the inn, which is regarded as THE HISTORIC HOME OF ROCK CLIMBING.

Napes Needle forms the centrepiece for the design of the badge of the world's premier rock climbing club, the FELL AND ROCK CLIMBING CLUB, which held its first meet at the Wastwater Hotel in 1907. Amongst its members past and present are EDWARD NORTON and HOWARD SOMERVELL of Mount Everest fame, SIR CHRIS BONINGTON, THE FIRST MAN TO CLIMB THE SOUTH FACE OF ANNAPURNA, and ALAN HINKES, THE

FIRST BRITON TO CLIMB THE 'EIGHT THOUSANDERS', the 14 mountains of the world over 8,000 metres.

Wasdale Head is also the starting point for one of the easier paths up to the summit of Scafell Pike.

Scafell Pike

SCAFELL PIKE is THE HIGHEST MOUNTAIN IN ENGLAND, at 3,210 feet (978 m). The summit belongs to the National Trust, donated in 1919 by Lord Leconfield as a memorial to the men of the Lake District 'who fell for God and King, for freedom, peace and right in the Great War'. In clear weather the view can stretch as far as the Mourne Mountains in Northern Ireland, Snowdonia in Wales, the Merrick, 69 miles (111 km) away in Scotland, and the Cheviot, 83 miles (134 km) away in Northumberland.

The least difficult and most popular routes up Scafell begin at Wasdale Head and Seathwaite Farm in Borrowdale.

The World's Biggest Liar

During the 19th century the Wastwater Hotel, now the Wasdale Head Inn, was run by a popular fellow called WILL RITSON (1808–90), who used to entertain his guests with tall tales of the Lakes, claiming for example that the turnips grown in Wasdale were so big, they could be hollowed out and used as sheep pens. Such was his skill and imagination that he became known as the WORLD'S BIGGEST LIAR, and now every year a competition is held in his honour in Wasdale to find his successor as the World's Biggest Liar. Competitors have five minutes to tell the most convincing lie without the use of props. Politicians and lawyers are considered professionals and are banned.

The south-west end of Wastwater is very different from the north-east end at Wasdale Head. Looking south, Wasdale softens into a gentle river valley of trees and fields falling leisurely towards the coast. Wastwater is the source of the RIVER IRT, which wiggles and burbles to the sea at Ravenglass.

Eskdale

Of Rats and Romans

ESKDALE is one of the few valleys in the Lake District without a lake, but enjoys a wealth of scenery as it descends from the high Hardknott Pass to the sands of Ravenglass. Despite a number of attractions, it is one of the quieter valleys.

Ravenglass

RAVENGLASS is CUMBERLAND'S OLDEST SEAPORT and consists of a breezy main street that straggles along the now sanded-up estuary where three rivers meet, the Irt, the Mite and the Esk. The Romans established an important naval base here in about AD 79, called GLANNAVENTA, and to protect it they built a fort, the final piece in a chain of fortifications that ran down the Cumberland coast as an extension of Hadrian's Wall.

The remains of the fort's bath house, now known as WALLS CASTLE, lie at the end of an avenue of trees leading south from Ravenglass, and make up one of Britain's largest and best-preserved Roman remains. Parts of the wall are 12 ft (3.7 m) high, THE HIGHEST SECTION OF DEFENSIVE ROMAN WALL STILL STANDING IN BRITAIN.

Lil' Ratty

The RAVENGLASS AND ESKDALE RAILWAY was built by a man named Ratcliffe and is known today as LIL' RATTY in his honour. It was opened in 1875 to transport iron ore from workings near Boot in Eskdale to the Furness railway at Ravenglass, and was THE FIRST NARROW-GAUGE RAILWAY IN ENGLAND.

Lil' Ratty runs for 7 miles (11 km) through the glorious countryside of Miterdale and Eskdale to Dalegarth, near BOOT, a little village that grew up to service the nearby iron ore mines.

Muncaster Castle

A 20-minute walk to the east of Ravenglass is MUNCASTER CASTLE, a grand battlemented pile dating from the early 13th century, which sits above the Esk on a height fortified by the Romans.

The original 14th-century pele tower was added to in the 19th century with a matching tower and later, in 1862, with work by Anthony Salvin. The result is spectacular, grey-pink and grim against a backdrop of sea and Lakeland fells – with beautiful gardens containing ONE OF THE LARGEST COLLECTIONS OF RHODODENDRONS IN EUROPE and a terrace walk described by John Ruskin as the 'GATEWAY TO PARADISE'.

Since at least as far back as 1208, Muncaster has been the home of the PENNINGTONS, who no doubt owe their long and successful occupancy to the 'LUCK OF MUNCASTER'.

The Luck of Muncaster

In 1464, during the Wars of the Roses, shepherds found Henry VI wandering on Muncaster Fell, after he had been defeated at the Battle of Hexham. A white monument on the slopes of Muncaster Fell just off the main road to the north east marks the place where he was discovered. The shepherds brought Henry to the castle and he was given shelter by Sir John Pennington, staying for nine days hidden in a room by the clock tower which is still there, identified as King Henry's Room. In return for their hospitality Henry gave the Penningtons a small, green, gold and enamel drinking bowl, telling his hosts that as long as the bowl remained unbroken the Penningtons would live and flourish at Muncaster. So far, the bowl, which is kept somewhere very secret and safe, is intact, and the family are still there.

Tom the Fool

Muncaster Castle is haunted by several ghosts, among them Henry VI, a decapitated carpenter, and Mary Bragg, hanged from the main gate by drunken youths. The most sinister apparition, however, is the ghost of Tom Skelton, otherwise known as TOM THE FOOL, who was a jester at the castle, one of the last, if not the last, court jester in England. His sense of humour was a bit unorthodox and ran to decapitating the above-mentioned carpenter and directing travellers looking for Ravenglass into quicksand down by the river. Tom the Fool still apparently gets up to his old tricks in the Tapestry Room.

Eskdale Mill

ESKDALE MILL is one of England's oldest water-powered corn mills and THE LAST WORKING MILL IN THE LAKE DISTRICT. The present mill dates back to 1578, but there has been a mill here probably since Roman times or before. The approach is over a 17th-century packhorse bridge across the WHILLAN BECK, which runs off the flanks of Scafell and has never been known to dry up.

Stanley Ghyll Force

STANLEY GHYLL FORCE, named after the Stanley family who lived at the ancient Dalegarth Hall, is one of Lakeland's most graceful falls, a shimmering white band that tumbles for 60 ft (18 m) into a deep, mossy ravine. The gorge is rich in plants, weeping ferns and ledges laden with rhododendrons, giving the whole place an almost tropical or oriental feel.

Hardknott

The village of Boot lies at the foot of the notorious HARDKNOTT PASS, which, along with Rosedale Chimney Bank in Yorkshire, is THE STEEPEST ROAD IN ENGLAND, with a gradient in some places of 1 in 3. The road wiggles upwards in a series of tight hairpin bends to a height of 1,289 ft (393 m) and is almost always closed in winter.

The present road follows the route of the Roman road from Ravenglass to the garrison at Ambleside, and is watched over by the Roman HARDKNOTT CASTLE or MEDIOBOGDUM, which must have been one of the loneliest and bleakest postings in the entire Roman Empire.

The fort was built in AD 120 on an undulating promontory overlooking Eskdale from a height of 700 ft (213 m) above sea level, and consists today of the remains of a granary, barracks, bath house and commandant's house, all in a huge square enclosure of some 3 acres (1.2 ha). From above, the fort looks as though it has been laid down on a crinkled bedspread.

Hardknott Castle is owned by the National Trust and run by English

Heritage. There is a small car park scooped out of a lay-by halfway down the hill, just below the fort, which is easy to miss – and it's too late to stop once you have missed it.

Duddon Valley

All hail, ye mountains! hail,
thou morning light!
Better to breathe upon this aery height
Than pass in needless sleep
from dream to dream:
Pure flow the verse, pure,
vigorous, free, and bright,
For Duddon, long-loved
Duddon is my theme!
WILLIAM WORDSWORTH

The sublime scenery of Lakeland's least-known valley inspired William Wordsworth to write 34 sonnets about the RIVER DUDDON'S journey to the sea. The Duddon begins that journey near the THREE SHIRES STONE at the top of WRYNOSE PASS, which marks the point where the three historic counties of Cumberland, Westmor-

land and Lancashire meet. It then rushes through a chasm, Wordsworth's 'miniature Niagara', under the picture-perfect packhorse bridge called BIRKS BRIDGE and on to form the boundary between Cumberland and the Furness district of Lancashire, all the way down to the wide Duddon Sands, where it enters the sea.

The highlight of the valley is the simple little 17th-century church of ST JOHN THE BAPTIST at ULPHA, nobly set on a high mound above the river, 'welcome as a star, that doth present its shining forehead through the peaceful rent of a black cloud diffused o'er half the sky', according to Wordsworth. Certainly the view from the churchyard, up towards the romantic ruins of Frith Hall, framed on the hilltop, induces a feeling of deep peace.

Well, I never knew this
about
THE WESTERN LAKES

ENNERDALE WATER can be seen in the closing scenes of Danny Boyle's 2002 film *28 Days Later*.

Buried amongst all the climbers in the tiny churchyard of St Olaf's at Wasdale Head is ALEXANDRINA WILSON, THE LAST TEACHER IN WASDALE, who died in 1947.

Five minutes' walk south of the summit of Scafell Pike is BROAD CRAG TARN, which stands at a height of 2,748 ft (838 m) and is THE HIGHEST BODY OF STANDING WATER IN ENGLAND.

Water from WASTWATER is used by the Sellafield nuclear waste processing facility.

The GOSFORTH CROSS in the churchyard of St Mary's, Gosforth, in south Wasdale, is THE OLDEST AND TALLEST

VIKING CROSS IN ENGLAND, 15 ft (4.6 m) tall and dating from the 10th century. Elaborate carvings depict scenes from Norse mythology.

RAVENGLASS IS THE ONLY COASTAL TOWN WITHIN THE LAKE DISTRICT NATIONAL PARK.

DRIGGS DUNES, near Ravenglass, is home to THE BIGGEST COLONY OF BLACK-HEADED GULLS IN EUROPE.

The grounds at MUNCASTER CASTLE contain the WORLD OWL CENTRE, home of the Owl Trust and ONE OF THE LARGEST COLLECTIONS OF OWLS IN THE WORLD, with 48 species including THE LARGEST, THE EUROPEAN EAGLE OWL, and THE SMALLEST, THE PYGMY AND SCOOP OWLS.

CONISTON

CONISTON WATER ✦ BRANTWOOD ✦ TARN HOWS ✦
WORLD RECORDS ✦ CONISTON VILLAGE ✦
OLD MAN OF CONISTON ✦ JOHN RUSKIN ✦
W.G. COLLINGWOOD ✦ ARTHUR RANSOME

Steam yacht *Gondola* – flagship of the National Trust fleet

Coniston Water

Of Ruskin and Records

CONISTON WATER IS THE THIRD LARGEST LAKE IN THE LAKE DISTRICT, 5½ miles (8.8 km) long, ½ mile (800 m) wide and 184 ft (56 m) deep.

Gondola

The most comfortable way to travel on Coniston Water is aboard BRITAIN'S OLDEST WORKING STEAM YACHT THE *GONDOLA*, the FLAGSHIP AND ONLY VESSEL OF THE NATIONAL TRUST FLEET. The original *Gondola* was constructed in 1859 for the Furness Railway, as a pleasure boat for tourists brought to Coniston Water by the railway. This she did for nearly 80 years until she was retired in 1936 and used as a houseboat at the south end of the lake. Left to rot in the 1960s, *Gondola* was recovered in the mid 1970s and rebuilt by Vickers at Barrow-in-Furness, and now plies the lake between Coniston village and Brantwood.

Gondola gave Arthur Ransome the idea for Captain Flint's houseboat in his children's novel *Swallows and Amazons*.

Brantwood – Part One

BRANTWOOD was the home of the social reformer and critic JOHN RUSKIN for nearly 30 years, and was where he died in 1900. When Ruskin bought the property in 1871 it was not much more than a large cottage, and he immediately set about extending and improving it, with particular regard to exploiting the view, regarded as the best on Coniston Water. He also built on extra accommodation for his beloved cousin Joan and a studio for Arthur Severn, her artist husband.

Since 1951 Brantwood has been owned and run as a museum by the Brantwood Trust, who have refurbished the house with memorabilia from Ruskin's vast collection of books, furniture and paintings, and in particular a mass of works by his favourite artist, J.M.W. Turner.

Ruskin was a keen gardener, and the gardens, running for over 1 mile (1.6 km) along the lake, have been restored to how they were in his time, with eight different types of plantations, ranging from moorland, ferns and herbs to azaleas, wild daffodil fields and Ruskin's own design the ZIG-ZAGGY, a walk made from plants through Dante's Purgatory to Paradise. The estate runs to 250 acres (101 ha), much of which is woodland – Brantwood means 'steep wood' – and there are walks and trails to various viewpoints and secret corners.

Tarn Hows

Gondola also calls at MONK CONISTON, from where there is a delightful walk to one of the Lake District's most picturesque and popular beauty spots, TARN HOWS. Despite blending in so well with the superb mountain scenery, and seeming so completely natural that it features in calendars and postcards as one of the archetypal Lakeland sights, Tarn Hows is a man-made wonder, a lake of unsurpassed loveliness created in the 19th century from three smaller tarns by Leeds MP James Garth Marshall of Monk Coniston Hall. The thick woodland of pine, spruce and larch that surrounds the tranquil waters provides an ideal

habitat for Lakeland's dwindling population of red squirrels.

Beatrix Potter purchased Tarn Hows from Marshall in 1929, and sold half the estate to the National Trust, bequeathing the other half to the Trust in her will.

World Records

Between 1939 and 1967 Coniston Water was the scene of a number of world water speed record attempts. Coniston was chosen because it has THE LONGEST STRAIGHT STRETCH OF DEEP WATER, CLEAR OF ISLANDS AND OTHER OBSTACLES, OF ANY ENGLISH LAKE.

In August 1939, SIR MALCOLM CAMPBELL (1885–1948) set a world water speed record of 141.7 mph (228 kph) on Coniston Water, in his boat *Bluebird K4*. Twelve years later, in 1951, his son DONALD CAMPBELL made an unsuccessful attempt to break the record on Coniston Water in the same boat.

Donald then developed a new boat, the *Bluebird K7*, in which he went on to set seven world water speed records, the first, 202.15 mph

(325.25 kph), on Ullswater in 1955, the last, 276.33 mph (446.61 kph) on Lake Dumbleyung in Perth, Australia, in 1964. He remains THE HOLDER OF THE HIGHEST NUMBER OF WORLD WATER SPEED RECORDS and is THE ONLY PERSON EVER TO HOLD BOTH THE WATER AND LAND SPEED RECORDS AT THE SAME TIME.

On 4 January 1967 Donald Campbell made an attempt on Coniston Water to break his own record by reaching 300 mph (483 kph) in *Bluebird K7*. His first run from north to south averaged 297 mph (478 kph), but on the return run *Bluebird* flipped over at some 303 mph (487.5 kph) and disintegrated. Campbell was killed instantly.

The wreckage of *Bluebird* was raised in 2000. Campbell's body was recovered in 2001 and buried in Coniston Cemetery, and there is a memorial to him, and to his mechanic Leo Villa, on the village green.

The tail fin of *Bluebird K7* and memorabilia of Donald Campbell, including his helmet, are on display in the Ruskin Museum in Coniston.

Coniston Village

CONISTON (King's Town) village is a typical Lakeland village with stone cottages, old pubs and hotels. Originally a scattering of farms and rural communities based around CONISTON HALL, a home of the Fleming family, it grew to serve the copper mines on the slopes of the Old Man of Coniston, and then later, with the arrival in 1859 of the Furness Railway, as a tourist centre. John Ruskin also popularised Coniston when he came to live across the water at Brantwood, and when he chose Coniston over Westminster Abbey as his last resting place.

The RUSKIN MUSEUM in Coniston has displays of Ruskin's life and works as well as the history of Coniston and the surrounding area.

Old Man of Coniston

Coniston and Coniston Water are overlooked by the OLD MAN OF CONISTON which, at 2,634 ft (803 m) high, is THE HIGHEST MOUNTAIN IN FURNESS and THE HIGHEST POINT IN THE COUNTY PALATINE OF LANCASHIRE (which still

exists). Being slightly apart from the main body of mountains it has one of the finest views, not only of the sea and distant features such as Blackpool Tower and the Isle of Man, but also of the Lake District fells themselves. The mountain's copper mines used to be amongst the largest in Britain, and there were also a number of slate mines and quarries, one of which, Bursting Stone Quarry, still operates, producing a much sought-after olive green slate.

John Ruskin
(1819–1900)

'Remember, the most beautiful things in the world are the most useless: peacocks and lilies, for instance'
JOHN RUSKIN

JOHN RUSKIN was one of the great figures of the Victorian era, a poet, artist, critic and conservationist. He believed that artists are at their best when inspired by the natural world, was a great admirer of the work of Turner and a champion of the emerging Pre-Raphaelites.

In architecture he held that the Gothic style best reflected the natural world, although he considered age and function to be equally important considerations in the value of a building, and believed that old buildings should be preserved as an organic part of the landscape.

He was also a social revolutionary and reformer, whose essays and writings had a huge influence on the thinking and institutions of the 19th century, particularly early members of the Labour movement. Amongst his radical ideas were a welfare state, a national health service, a minimum wage, old age pensions, public libraries and art galleries, and 'green' policies for mitigating the threat of pollution and greenhouse gases.

Ruskin's personal life was not an unqualified success. His marriage to Effie Gray was annulled after seven years on the grounds of his refusal to consummate it, and the fact that Effie had eloped with one of Ruskin's protégés, John Millais, whom she later married.

Ruskin's Inspirations

The son of a rich wine merchant, founder of the company that became Allied Domecq, Ruskin was born and raised in London, but his first real memory in life was of a visit to the beauty spot of

FRIAR'S CRAG on Derwentwater when he was five years old, an occasion that he recalled as 'the creation of the world for me'.

And it was another visit to the Lake District that inspired the young Ruskin to first write down his thoughts and impressions, when he and his parents returned to Keswick for a holiday in 1830, and he wrote about a trip to Coniston in a highly regarded poem called 'Iteriad'. On that same holiday Ruskin saw his hero the poet WILLIAM WORDSWORTH in RYDAL CHURCH. One Ruskin's first professional publications, written a few years later, was called *The Poetry of Architecture*, in which he espoused Wordsworth's argument that buildings should be sympathetic with their environment and constructed out of local materials.

Coniston Hall

There is a picture in *The Poetry of Architecture* of CONISTON HALL, a medieval home of the Fleming family on the western shore of Coniston Water.

Ruskin sketched the hall in 1837 during one of his trips to the Lake District as a young man, and used it to illustrate a discussion on chimneys, for which Coniston Hall is famous. Commenting that chimneys are often eyesores, he says they are 'sometimes attended with good effect, as in the old building called Coniston Hall on the shores of Coniston Water, whose distant outline is rendered light and picturesque by the size and shape of its chimneys . . .'

Coniston Hall was Ruskin's idea of the perfect Lakeland architecture. The house, which had been built originally in 1270 and then rebuilt in the 16th century, is sturdy and rough-hewn, and Ruskin thought it blended supremely with the rugged scenery. It also had a dash of romance about it, for in the 16th century the courtly poet-soldier SIR PHILIP SIDNEY had lived there for a while with his sister Mary. Little did young Ruskin imagine that one day he would be able to see such a place from his own study window across the lake.

Brantwood – Part Two

Many cherished memories made Ruskin determined to return and live in the Lake District one day, and in 1871, at the age of 52, when his reputation had been made, he realised his dream and acquired BRANTWOOD, a cottage on the eastern shore of Conis-

ton Water, where he lived for the rest of his life, nearly 30 years. Almost the first thing he did was to build a turret on to the side of the house from where he could look out over Coniston Water to the Coniston hills, a view he described as 'on the whole, the finest view I know in Cumberland or Lancashire'.

Brantwood became the place where Ruskin could write and relax, where 'Morning breaks as I write, among those Coniston fells . . .', and where he received many distinguished visitors, amongst them Charles Darwin, Holman Hunt, Sir Edward Burne-Jones and the children's illustrator Kate Greenaway. He filled the house with art treasures, medieval manuscripts, books and a fine collection of minerals.

Ruskin died in 1900 in his bedroom at Brantwood, his last memory being of his beloved view

across Coniston Water and the distant outline of Coniston Hall to the blue Coniston hills beyond. He was buried in a quiet corner of the churchyard at St Andrew's Church in Coniston village, his grave marked by a tall Celtic cross carved with symbols depicting his life and work, designed by his friend W.G. Collingwood.

W.G. Collingwood
(1854–1932)

William Gershom Collingwood, born in Liverpool, was an accomplished author, artist and antiquary. He studied under John Ruskin at Oxford University, and after visiting Ruskin at Brantwood in 1873, decided to move to the Lake District himself. In 1883 he married and settled at Lanehead, beside Coniston Water, about 1 mile (1.6 km) from Brantwood. He eventually became Ruskin's assistant and secretary, helping to run Brantwood, editing his texts and writing a biography of Ruskin in 1893.

When Ruskin died in 1900, Collingwood gathered together as many Ruskin mementoes as he could find and set up an exhibition in Coniston, which evolved into the Ruskin Museum. Collingwood himself, and his wife Edith, are buried near Ruskin in St Andrew's churchyard in Coniston village.

Arthur Ransome
(1884–1967)

As a boy Arthur Ransome, who was born in Leeds, spent many happy times in the Lake District, going to school in Windermere and spending the holidays at Nibthwaite at the southern end of Coniston Water. Here he met and became friends with W.G. Collingwood and his family, who lived at Lanehead at the north end of Coniston Water. The Collingwood children taught Ransome how to sail on their father's fishing boat called *Swallow*, and Ransome would later use the names of some of Collingwood's grandchildren for the Walker children in his stories.

After an unhappy marriage, Ransome escaped to Russia where, in 1917, he reported for the London newspapers on the Russian Revolution, sending back information on the Bolshevik leaders Lenin and Trotsky to the British government. Ransome got to know Lenin and Trotsky well, and even claimed to have beaten Lenin at chess. Leon Trotsky's secretary Evgenia became Ransome's second wife, and in 1925 they settled in the Lake District at Low Ludderburn in the Winster valley, south of Windermere, where he began writing *Swallows and Amazons* in 1929. His stories are set around Coniston and Windermere, and there are special trips on both lakes that visit some of the locations used in the books.

Arthur Ransome and Evgenia, who spent their final years in a house called HILL TOP in HAVERTHWAITE, are buried in the hillside churchyard of ST PAUL'S at RUSLAND. Their gravestone stands, 'with the sound of the wind in the pine needles', beneath a tree in a spot they chose themselves.

Many of the locations in the *Swallows and Amazons* books are an amalgam of more than one place. For instance 'that great lake in the north' is both Coniston Water and Windermere. PEEL ISLAND on Coniston Water becomes Wildcat Island, where in the books the Walker children sail to and set up camp. As a boy Ransome and the Collingwood children would land on Peel Island and picnic there. In the book *Swallowdale* the OLD MAN OF CONISTON becomes Mount Kanchenjunga. BANK GROUND FARM, across the lake from Coniston, near to the Collingwoods' house, is Holly Howe, where the Walker family lived. The farm was used in the 1974 film of *Swallows and Amazons* starring Virginia McKenna and Donald Fraser. It is now a B&B.

Well, I never knew this
about
CONISTON

The CONISTON BREWING COMPANY produces a range of local ales, including one called OLD MAN ALE and another called BLUEBIRD ALE, on sale at the 400-year-old Black Bull Inn, which featured in the 1988 BBC film *Across the Lake*, starring Anthony Hopkins as world speed record holder Donald Campbell.

A team is attempting to restore Donald Campbell's *Bluebird K7* for permanent display in the Ruskin Museum in Coniston. They are hoping to give it a final run on Coniston Water in 2011, and have already got permission to break the 10 mph (16 kph) speed limit in force on the lake for the occasion.

JOHN RUSKIN was responsible for introducing the May Day ceremony of children dancing around the maypole with ribbons.

THE FIRST ARTHUR RANSOME CLUB IN THE WORLD was formed in Tokyo, Japan, in 1987.

There is an ARTHUR RANSOME ROOM in the MUSEUM OF LAKELAND LIFE at Abbot Hall in Kendal, where you can see a reconstruction of Ransome's study, complete with his chess set, many of his drawings, and the type-writer on which he wrote many of his books.

The two traditional timber launches run on Coniston Water by the Coniston Launch company are called *RUSKIN* and *RANSOME*.

Coniston Launch

North Furness

Wray Castle, where Beatrix Potter first fell in love with the Lake District

Furness

Once a Red Rose

Furness is a peninsula that lies in what is now South Cumbria but before 1974 was a detached part of Lancashire. To the west it is bordered by Duddon Sands and the Duddon Valley, to the north by the River Brathay and to the south and east by Windermere, Morecambe Bay and the Isle of Walney.

Esthwaite Water

One morning . . . by Esthwaite's Lake,
. . . Life was sweet, I knew not why
WILLIAM WORDSWORTH

Little ESTHWAITE WATER, some 2 miles (3.2 km) long and 80 ft (24 m) deep, lies between the Lake District's two busiest lakes, Coniston Water and Windermere, and is consequently rather overlooked and pleasantly peaceful. It is a riot of water lilies in summer and very popular with fishermen in winter, particularly well stocked with trout and pike.

William Wordsworth used to take long walks by Esthwaite Water while he was attending Hawkshead Grammar School, and mentions the lake in his autobiographical poem 'The Prelude'.

HAWKSHEAD GRAMMAR SCHOOL was founded in 1585 by EDWIN SANDYS, Archbishop of York, who was born in 1519 in the lovely old ESTHWAITE HALL, which still stands on the western shore. It still belongs to the Sandys family, but it is now run as a bed and breakfast establishment, and the family live about 3 miles (5 km) to the south in GRAYTHWAITE HALL, which has delightful gardens open to the public in the summer months.

Hawkshead

'Prettiest village in the Lake District'

HAWKSHEAD, which sits at the head of Esthwaite Water, was founded in Norse times and later belonged to

Furness Abbey. All that remains of Hawkshead Hall, the medieval manorial farm, is the 13th-century gatehouse, which had a court room above it and is now known as the COURTHOUSE. It lies just outside the present village to the north.

Today, Hawkshead is one of the Lake District's show villages, much of it owned by the National Trust and wonderfully unspoiled, with cobbled squares, winding alleyways and colourful houses with overhanging gables.

The impressive St Michael's Church stands on a mound above the village, commanding tremendous views. Until the 20th century it was whitewashed and visible for miles around. Inside are the tombs of Edwin Sandys's parents, William and Margaret.

Hawkshead Grammar School

After his mother died, the poet William Wordsworth attended HAWKSHEAD GRAMMAR SCHOOL from

1779 until 1787, and the wooden desk where he carved his name can still be seen in the schoolroom, THE OLDEST EXAMPLE OF WORDSWORTH'S HAND THAT SURVIVES. One of the teachers at the school while Wordsworth was there was Edward Christian, older brother of Fletcher Christian, leader of the mutineers on the *Bounty*. Like Wordsworth, the Christians were born in Cockermouth, and the families probably knew each other.

While at the school, Wordsworth lived in the centre of Hawkshead in ANN TYSON'S COTTAGE, an adorable little 17th-century building with stone steps leading up by the door. The cottage is now used for self-catering accommodation, and there is a plaque to Wordsworth on the wall.

Another notable student of Hawkshead Grammar School was LORD BROUGHAM (1778–1868), scion of a prominent Westmorland family, who went on to become Lord Chancellor and to champion both the 1832 Reform Act and the 1833 Slavery Abolition Act. He also invented the one-horse closed carriage, known as the brougham, and holds the record for THE LONGEST SPEECH EVER GIVEN IN THE HOUSE OF COMMONS, just over six hours.

The Grammar School closed in 1909 and is now maintained as a museum.

Just Pottering

In Main Street, the BEATRIX POTTER GALLERY occupies the former office of Potter's husband WILLIAM HEELIS, who was a local solicitor. The gallery displays many of Beatrix Potter's original watercolours and sketches.

Beatrix Potter based her character Johnny Town-Mouse on Hawkshead's village doctor, Dr Parsons.

Wray Castle

A Position of Trust

WRAY CASTLE is a massive embattled Victorian Gothic pile overlooking Windermere that was built in the 1840s for DR JAMES DAWSON, a retired surgeon from Liverpool, one of the first doctors admitted to the Royal College of Surgeons, and a man blessed with a rich wife. Her fortune came from gin, which is ironic because after she had taken one look at the castle and point blank refused to live there, the architect of the place, H.P. HORNER, drank himself to death – most probably with gin.

Mrs Dawson was a strangely ungrateful woman, for Wray Castle is a heavenly place. The rooms are beautifully designed and decorated, and the luscious gardens give ravishing and unforgettable views across Windermere to Ambleside and the mountains beyond, and to the Langdale Pikes, views that make most visitors never want to leave.

These were the views that Wordsworth celebrated by planting a mulberry tree in the garden in 1845 (it is still there), the views that made Beatrix Potter want to start drawing when she came here on holiday with her parents, and the views that made the Vicar of Wray, Canon Rawnsley, strive to save it all by setting up a national trust.

The castle is in fact now owned by the National Trust, but open only sporadically. The grounds are always open.

Canon Hardwicke Drummond Rawnsley
(1851–1920)

'It is no exaggeration to say ...
that England would be a much duller
and less healthy and happy country
if he had not lived and worked'
Obituary, *THE TIMES*

HARDWICKE DRUMMOND RAWNSLEY was born in Shiplake, near Henley in Oxfordshire, the son of a clergyman. At Oxford University he came under the influence of John Ruskin, and in 1877, at the young age of 26, moved to the Lake District, not far from Ruskin at Brantwood, to become the Vicar of Wray, near Windermere, on the estate of his cousin Preston Rawnsley of Wray Castle.

Rawnsley instantly fell in love with the Lake District, married a local girl, Edith Fletcher from Ambleside, and settled down to his new life, visiting

Ruskin and exploring the places made famous by the poetry of William Wordsworth.

In 1883 he became involved in a battle to stop a railway being built from Buttermere to Keswick, which he thought would ruin the landscape, and spurred on by the success of this campaign formed the Lake District Defence Society, which included in its membership the Duke of Westminster, Matthew Arnold and the poets Robert Browning and Alfred, Lord Tennyson, a friend of Rawnsley's father. Their first success was to stop a proposed railway running through Ennerdale.

In 1883 Rawnsley was appointed Vicar of Crosthwaite, at Keswick, where he became something of a big wheel in the community, founding Keswick School of Industrial Art, becoming a Canon of Carlisle Cathedral, a county councillor and, above all, a champion of the Lake District, always ready to defend it against pollution, industrialisation and ugly development.

He became alarmed that private landowners were able to shut footpaths and restrict access to beauty spots, and determined to put into practice a dream that both Wordsworth and Ruskin had put forward, to set up some kind of organisation that could purchase such places to preserve them and open them up to the public.

He joined forces with his friends the social campaigner Octavia Hill and a lawyer, Sir Robert Hunter, solicitor to the Commons Preservation Society, and they had a meeting at the Duke of Westminster's London house to discuss setting up a national trust for the preservation of places of historic interest or natural beauty. In 1895 the dream was realised when the National Trust was founded, with the Duke of Westminster as the first president and Rawnsley as the first secretary, a position he held until his death in 1920.

In 1917 Rawnsley retired from Crosthwaite after 34 years and bought Allan Bank, the house in Grasmere where Wordsworth had lived briefly after moving out of Dove Cottage. He died there in 1920 and is buried in the churchyard at Crosthwaite. Allan Bank he left to the National Trust.

National Trust

A Vicar's Bequest

The Lake District is THE BIRTHPLACE OF THE NATIONAL TRUST, the FIRST AND LARGEST ORGANISATION OF ITS

KIND IN THE WORLD. The seductive landscapes and scenery of the Lakes inspired first William Wordsworth at Grasmere, and then John Ruskin at Brantwood, to dream of some system that could preserve such beauty and make it accessible to future generations for ever. Canon Rawnsley, Vicar of Crosthwaite, aided by social reformer Octavia Hill and preservation lawyer Sir Robert Hunter, made that dream come true with the founding in 1895 of the NATIONAL TRUST FOR THE PRESERVATION OF PLACES OF HISTORIC INTEREST OR NATURAL BEAUTY.

In 1902 the BRANDLEHOW ESTATE, some 100 acres (40 ha) of woodland and fields on the western shore of Derwentwater, became available, and Rawnsley launched an appeal for funds to buy it. The money was raised and Brandlehow became THE NATIONAL TRUST'S FIRST-EVER PURCHASE.

It was due to Canon Rawnsley's influence and friendship that Beatrix Potter left a considerable bequest of land to the National Trust on her death in 1943.

In 1981 Ralph Bankes gifted the entire Kingston Lacy estate in Dorset to the National Trust, the largest bequest in the Trust's history. The Bankes fortune was built on their profits from the Borrowdale graphite mine (*see* Borrowdale), on land which they acquired in 1625.

Today the National Trust owns about a quarter of the Lake District, 124,000 acres (50,200 ha), 91 farms, six of the major lakes, including the deepest, Wastwater, many of the peaks, including the highest, Scafell Pike, beauty spots such as Tarn Hows, the Langdale valleys, Borrowdale, Buttermere, Aira Force, and numerous properties such as Cartmel Priory gatehouse, Dalton Castle, Hill Top, Sizergh Castle, Townend and Dove Cottage.

In 1907 the National Trust was granted the unique privilege of being able to declare its lands and properties inalienable, meaning that they cannot ever be sold, mortgaged or developed for the rest of time, thus ensuring that some of the most beautiful countryside and buildings in England will be saved for the enjoyment of future generations for ever.

Wordsworth and Ruskin would be proud.

Beatrix Potter

(1866–1943)

BEATRIX POTTER was born in London, and first visited the Lake District in 1882 when she was 16. She came with her parents to spend the summer at Wray Castle and was enchanted by the Lakeland scenery, spending as much time as she could exploring and sketching the animals and flowers she

discovered. In this she was greatly encouraged by Hardwicke Rawnsley, the Vicar of Wray, who became great friends with her parents and a regular visitor to the castle.

Over the next few years the Potters spent many further holidays in the Lake District, mainly at Lingholm and Fawe Park on Derwentwater, where Beatrix made drawings of the vegetable gardens that would become Mr McGregor's garden, and found the settings for many of her subsequent books.

Hardwicke Rawnsley moved from Wray to Crosthwaite, but continued to visit the Potters whenever they were in the Lake District, and was very taken with Beatrix's drawings. He suggested she should write and illustrate her own books, and in the summer of 1901 she sat down and wrote about a little rabbit called Peter, based on a story she had told in a letter to a friend some years before. She had 250 copies made in black and white and finally, with the help of Rawnsley, she found a publisher, Frederick Warne. They brought out a colour edition of *Peter Rabbit*

in 1902, which became one of the best-selling and best-loved children's books of all time.

With the royalties from *Peter Rabbit*, Beatrix was finally able to buy her own home in her beloved Lake District, and in 1905 she acquired HILL TOP, a small 17th-century farmhouse in Sawrey, on a hill above the western shore of Windermere. She used Hill Top as a bolt hole to get away from London and to write, and many of her characters were conceived there, Tom Kitten, Samuel Whiskers and Jemima Puddleduck amongst them. The house itself is ordinary, but there is much enjoyment to be had from trying to spot furniture or views that appear in the books – the dresser, for instance, is in *The Tailor of Gloucester*, the bedroom in *Two Bad Mice*, and the staircase will look familiar to readers of *The Tale of Samuel Whiskers*.

In 1909 Beatrix bought CASTLE FARM across the road from Hill Top, and in 1913 married WILLIAM HEELIS, the solicitor from Hawkshead who helped her with her property

transactions. They made Castle Farm their main home and kept Hill Top as a writing retreat for Beatrix.

Apart from being a brilliant illustrator, Beatrix Potter was a fine businesswoman, and one of the first writers to market and franchise herself and her characters – she patented Peter Rabbit early on in 1903.

As the royalties rolled in she was able to buy further properties, and in 1923, to save it from the threat of development, she purchased a large sheep farm on the slopes of the Kirkstone Pass called TROUTBECK PARK FARM, and here built up an admired flock of Herdwick sheep, a small, hardy breed of sheep indigenous to the Lake District. She made Troutbeck the setting for her *Fairy Caravan* stories.

In 1930 Beatrix bought the MONK CONISTON ESTATE, which included TARN HOWS, and in that same year she wrote her last story, *The Tale of Little Pig Robinson*, and began to concentrate on her farming instead.

When she died in 1943, Beatrix Potter left 4,000 acres (1,620 ha) of the Lake District, 14 farms and all her flocks of Herdwick sheep to the National Trust, the brainchild of her dear friend Canon Hardwicke Rawnsley. On those wonderful summer holidays of her youth, not only had Rawnsley encouraged her drawing and given her the confidence to pursue her dreams, but had also opened her eyes to the need to

preserve and nurture the landscape she found so inspiring – she became the National Trust's greatest benefactor.

Leven Valley

Red, White and Blue

White

The white waters of the fast-flowing RIVER LEVEN, which drains Windermere, in days of old provided power for a huge variety of mills, making the Leven Valley in its time almost as important an industrial area as Coalbrookdale in Shropshire. In Tudor times there was a corn mill at BACKBARROW established by the monks of Cartmel Priory, and even earlier there were mills working there on behalf of the monks of Furness Abbey.

Red

At LOW WOOD, just down the road, there are still occasional signs of a red

---

Places in the Lake District associated with Beatrix Potter

WRAY CASTLE, now National Trust, gardens open to the public.

DERWENTWATER. Mr McGregor's Garden (Lingholm, Fawe Park and Holehird). ST HERBERT'S ISLAND, Owl Island in *The Tale of Squirrel Nutkin.*

NEWLANDS VALLEY, the setting for *The Tale of Mrs Tiggywinkle.*

HILL TOP, SAWREY. Left exactly as it was when Beatrix lived there. Open to the public and one of the most visited literary shrines in the world. National Trust.

TOWER BANK ARMS, just below Hill Top in Sawrey. Features in *The Tale of Jemima Puddleduck.* National Trust.

MOSS ECCLES TARN, a short walk from Hill Top. Here Beatrix would go rowing, in a boat now to be seen at the Steamboat Museum at Windermere. The water lilies on the tarn inspired the story of Jeremy Fisher, the gentleman frog. National Trust.

HAWKSHEAD. BEATRIX POTTER GALLERY, with original watercolours and sketches housed in the offices of her husband William Heelis.

AMBLESIDE. THE ARMITT LIBRARY displays some of Beatrix Potter's original natural history watercolours.

BOWNESS-ON-WINDERMERE. THE WORLD OF BEATRIX POTTER, with recreations of her characters and stories.

---

rust left behind by the ironworks which operated there until the 1940s. It was run during the 18th century by ISAAC WILKINSON, father of John 'Iron-Mad' Wilkinson (*see* Lindale). This was THE LAST IRONWORKS IN ENGLAND TO SMELT IRON ORE WITH CHARCOAL, and the remains of THE BLAST FURNACE, THE LAST SURVIVOR OF ITS KIND IN ENGLAND, can still be seen. There is now a hydro-electric scheme here which contributes power to the National Grid.

Blue

By 1790 Backbarrow had three cotton mills, which in 1816 were at the centre

of a scandal when a parliamentary investigation uncovered evidence of the misuse of child labour. One of the mills was destroyed by fire in 1856, and the other two were eventually taken over by the BRITISH ULTRAMARINE COMPANY for the manufacture of ultramarine and other blues used in hand-washing laundry to make it white. Reckitt's took over the mills in 1925 and they became known as the DOLLY BLUE MILLS after the company's most famous product, although Dolly Blue was never actually manufactured there. While the Blue Mills were in production most of Backbarrow, the River Leven and certainly all the mill workers were stained blue. The Blue Mills ceased production in 1981 because the introduction of automatic washing machines led to a collapse in the demand for washing blue, and the mill buildings have been converted into a luxury hotel. Backbarrow may no longer be blue but those days are remembered in the hotel's Blue Works Bar.

Well, I never knew this *about*

NORTH FURNESS

GRIZEDALE FOREST near Hawkshead is THE LARGEST FOREST IN THE LAKE DISTRICT. It was also THE FIRST FOREST WHERE THE FORESTRY COMMISSION SOUGHT TO PROVIDE RECREATIONAL FACILITIES. To this end Grizedale offers, amongst other things, a theatre-in-the-forest, an assault course, a mountain bike trail and a display of sculptures in wood, forming THE LARGEST EXHIBITION OF WOOD SCULPTURE IN BRITAIN.

The proudest possession of the church-yard at FINSTHWAITE, near Lakeside, is the gravestone of CLEMENTINA SOBIESKI DOUGLAS (1747–71), known as the 'Cumbrian Princess', and reputed to be the daughter of Bonnie Prince Charlie by his mistress Clementina Walkinshaw.

The LAKESIDE AND HAVERTHWAITE RAILWAY is a heritage railway that was rescued by enthusiasts in 1970. It operates steam trains on a branch line of the old Furness Railway for 3½ miles (5.6 km) along the Leven Valley, from Haverthwaite, through Newby Bridge to Lakeside. Their flagship locomotive, FR 0-4-0 No. 20, was built in 1863, and is BRITAIN'S OLDEST WORKING STANDARD-GAUGE STEAM LOCOMOTIVE.

Before the local government reorganisation of 1974, Furness was a detached part of Lancashire, known as Lancashire North of the Sands. Today it is in Cumbria, although it still belongs to the County Palatine of Lancashire.

In 1487 SIR THOMAS BROUGHTON rode out from BROUGHTON TOWER in BROUGHTON-IN-FURNESS to join the forces of the pretender LAMBERT SIMNEL, who had landed on Piel Island at the start of his unsuccessful quest to seize the crown of Henry VII. Sir Thomas was killed at the subsequent Battle of Stoke in June.

DUDDON IRON WORKS, near Broughton-in-Furness, operated from 1736 to 1866, and the remains form THE MOST COMPLETE SURVIVING EXAMPLE OF AN IRONWORKS SITE WITH CHARCOAL-FIRED BLAST FURNACE IN BRITAIN.

Beatrix Potter's father, RUPERT POTTER, WAS THE FIRST LIFE MEMBER OF THE NATIONAL TRUST.

South Furness

LINDALE ✦ DALTON-IN-FURNESS ✦ GEORGE ROMNEY ✦
FURNESS ABBEY ✦ PIEL CASTLE ✦
BARROW-IN-FURNESS ✦ ULVERSTON

Cartmel Priory, with England's only diagonal tower

Lindale-in-Cartmel

Birthplace of the Iron Boat

LINDALE-IN-CARTMEL sits on a steep hill looking over the rooftops of Grange-over-Sands towards Morecambe Bay. In the river meadows below the village is a fine Georgian house, CASTLE HEAD, which was built by JOHN 'IRON-MAD' WILKINSON after he moved to Lindale in 1750. The surrounding lands were marshy and prone to flooding and Wilkinson erected a huge embankment to keep the sea at bay, as well as developing new ways of draining the peaty soil and planting trees to bind the land together.

John Wilkinson
(1728–1808)

JOHN 'IRON-MAD' WILKINSON was born near Workington, the son of an ironworker, and grew to be the most successful and innovative ironmonger of the Industrial Revolution. Among his inventions was a cylinder boring machine that firstly made cannons safer to fire, more accurate and with a longer range, and secondly helped improve James Watt's steam engines, with the result that for 20 years Wilkinson was the sole manufacturer of steam engines for Boulton & Watt. In 1779 Wilkinson supplied the iron for the world's first iron bridge over the River Severn in Shropshire.

In 1786 Lindale was the setting for THE MAIDEN VOYAGE OF THE WORLD'S FIRST IRON BOAT, when Wilkinson tried out a scale model of an iron boat he had designed on the River Winster at Castle Head. Everyone predicted the boat would sink, but it dumbfounded them all by floating, and the following year Wilkinson launched THE WORLD'S FIRST FULL-SIZE IRON BOAT on the River Severn. He also made THE WORLD'S FIRST IRON PULPIT.

When he died John Wilkinson was buried in an iron coffin in the grounds of Castle Head, beneath a huge 40-ft (12 m) tall iron obelisk he had made himself, with his portrait in relief on the side. The next owners of the house thought the obelisk an eyesore, so it was knocked down and thrown into the under-growth. Wilkinson's coffin

was dug up and reburied somewhere in Lindale Church, the exact site of his grave long lost. The obelisk was eventually recovered and put up beside the village crossroads where it can be seen today.

Castle Head is now a centre for field studies.

Dalton-in-Furness

An Unexpected Castle

DALTON-IN-FURNESS looks at first sight like an attractive but quite ordi-nary little town, and it comes as quite a shock, when pottering about the cottages and cobbles of the pretty market square, to suddenly run up against an immense and very forbid-ding grey pele tower. Dalton, as it happens, was the medieval capital of Furness, and the market and judicial centre for Furness Abbey, and so Dalton Castle was built to protect the town, along with the abbey and its approaches.

Today the austere, four-square,

14th-century castle, in its incongruous setting, is run by the National Trust, and houses exhibitions of local history and local hero George Romney.

George Romney
(1734–1802)

GEORGE ROMNEY was born in Beckside, Dalton, the son of a cabinet-maker. His skill as an artist emerged in the drawings of ornaments and furniture he did while helping his father, and at 21 he went to Kendal to learn painting. He set up his own studio two years later, and quickly gained a following with his portraits of prominent Lakeland figures.

In 1762 Romney went to London, leaving his wife and children behind, and established a thriving business painting portraits of wealthy aristocrats and their families, becoming at his peak more fashionable than Sir Joshua Reynolds or Thomas Gainsborough. His portrait of William Pitt the Younger hangs in No. 10 Downing Street. Later, however, Romney's infatuation with the notorious Emma Hamilton, Lord Nelson's mistress,

who became his Muse, and of whom he painted some 60 portraits, somewhat damaged his reputation as a serious artist.

After nearly 40 years in London Romney returned to spend his final years with his wife in Kendal, and he is buried in the churchyard of St Mary's in Dalton, tucked away up a narrow lane off the market square. Although he was never a member of the Royal Academy, George Romney is today recognised as one of the most brilliant and influential artists of the late 18th century.

Furness Abbey

Romantic Ruins

The resplendent rose-pink ruins of Furness Abbey overflow the leafy green 'Vale of Deadly Nightshade' on the edge of Barrow-in-Furness. Founded in 1123 by the future King Stephen, Furness grew into a rich and powerful Cistercian house, second only to Fountains Abbey in Yorkshire, with vast interests in the Norse region of Sodor and the Isle of Man. Sodor is Norse for the southern isles, which is how the Norwegians used to refer to what are now the Hebrides. A 'King of Mann and the Isles' is buried at Furness, along with several Bishops of Sodor and Man, from an archaic bishopric that nonetheless still exists today.

In 1322 Robert the Bruce was entertained at Furness by the Abbot, John Cockerham, in a partially successful effort to prevent the Scottish king from sacking the abbey.

Furness Abbey was the first major abbey to dissolve voluntarily at the Reformation, fearful of being charged with treason for having taken part in the Pilgrimage of Grace in 1536, a northern uprising against the Dissolution of the Monasteries.

In the 19th century the ruins of Furness Abbey were imbued with romance in William Wordsworth's autobiographical poem 'The Prelude', and were also sketched by Turner.

Piel Castle

King of the Castle

Rising out of the distant sea against a backdrop of sand-dunes and sky, the huge keep of PIEL CASTLE makes a picturesque ruin. Where Dalton Castle once guarded the landward approaches to Furness Abbey, so did Piel Castle keep watch over the sea route to the monks' lands in Ireland and the Isle of Man. It sits on the tip of PIEL ISLAND at the mouth of the deep-water harbour of Barrow-in-Furness, and dates from the time of Edward III, when he gave the Furness monks permission to fortify their house on the island. In 1487 the 12-year-old Yorkist Pretender Lambert Simnel landed on Piel Island, with 2,000 men who had been assembled in Ireland, at the start of his unsuccessful campaign to win the throne of Henry VII.

Today Piel Castle is run by English Heritage, and the island has only one inhabitant, the landlord of the 300-year-old Ship Inn, who receives with his job the title of the KING OF PIEL, in caustic homage to Lambert Simnel. Each new landlord is crowned in a ceremony that involves having alcohol poured over his head, and has to promise to be a 'free drinker, a smoker and a lover of the female sex'. The inn is popular, not surprisingly, with yachtsmen and fishermen, as well as the visitors to Piel Castle who come across on the Roa Island ferry during the summer months.

Barrow-in-Furness

Steel and Submarines

BARROW-IN-FURNESS was a small fishing village until the mid 19th century, when speculator HENRY SCHNEIDER discovered huge iron ore deposits on the Furness peninsula and, along with SIR JAMES RAMSDEN, built the FURNESS RAILWAY to bring the ore to the harbour. The two men then constructed a blast furnace at Barrow, which by 1876 had become THE BIGGEST STEELWORKS IN THE WORLD. The population of Barrow increased from 700 in 1851 to 47,000 in 1881.

At the same time the men decided to use some of the steel they were producing to make ships, and the BARROW SHIPBUILDING COMPANY came into being. In 1897 it was taken over by the Sheffield steel firm of VICKERS, and is now THE BUSIEST SHIPYARD IN ENGLAND, complete with THE LARGEST COVERED SHIPBUILDING HALL IN EUROPE. Amongst famous warships built in Barrow are *MIKASA*, the Japanese flagship during the 1905 Russo-Japanese War, and the aircraft-carrier HMS *INVINCIBLE*, which found fame during the Falklands War. Barrow became synonymous with submarine manufacture, producing THE ROYAL NAVY'S FIRST-EVER SUBMARINE *HOLLAND I* in 1901, and BRITAIN'S FIRST NUCLEAR SUBMARINE HMS *DREADNOUGHT* in 1960.

The last steelworks in Barrow closed in 1983, and shipbuilding is now the town's major employer. All of Britain's Trident nuclear submarines were built at Barrow.

Ulverston

Birthplace of Comedy

The pleasant market town of ULVERSTON was the birthplace of comic genius and silent movie star STAN LAUREL, the thin half of the fabulous Laurel and Hardy duo. He was born STANLEY JEFFERSON in a small house in Argyle Street on 16 June 1890. A statue of Laurel and Hardy stands outside the Coronation Hall, and Ulverston is today the home of THE

WORLD'S ONLY LAUREL AND HARDY MUSEUM, which houses THE BIGGEST COLLECTION OF LAUREL AND HARDY MEMORABILIA IN THE WORLD. Their films are shown in a small cinema throughout the day.

Hoad Monument

Overlooking Ulverston from the top of nearby Hoad Hill, and a landmark for many miles around, is the HOAD MONUMENT, built in 1850 as a tribute to SIR JOHN BARROW, who was born in a small cottage in Dragley Beck, Ulverston, in 1764. The cottage still stands, on Priory Road.

The monument is built in the style of Smeaton's Eddystone Lighthouse, and is 100 ft (30.5 m) tall. Visitors may climb 122 steps to a viewing room near the top from where it is possible on a clear day to see Morecambe Bay, the Yorkshire Dales, the Lakeland Fells, Blackpool Tower and Snowdonia.

Sir John Barrow
(1764–1848)

SIR JOHN BARROW was Second Secretary to the Admiralty from 1804 until 1845. He oversaw the Battle of Trafalgar, was the last man to shake the hand of Lord Nelson as the Admiral stepped aboard HMS *Victory*, and was responsible for exiling Napoleon Bonaparte to the island of St Helena. He helped to establish the Royal Geographical Society, promoted a number of Arctic explorations, including those of John Ross, William Parry and John Franklin, and is commemorated by BARROW POINT on the northern tip of Alaska and BARROW STRAIT in Northern Canada.

Swarthmoor Hall

In fields outside Ulverston stands Elizabethan SWARTHMOOR HALL, its grey, austere appearance softened by a garden full of flowers and trees. This is possibly the most important Quaker building that exists, for here came GEORGE FOX in 1652, not long after

he had seen his vision on Pendle Hill, and this was the house in which he lived in those rare times when he was not travelling and preaching – or in gaol.

Swarthmoor Hall was the home of JUDGE THOMAS FELL, and while Fell was away George Fox converted the judge's wife MARGARET to his Quaker views. Fell, while not converted himself, smiled indulgently upon Fox and allowed him to use Swarthmoor Hall as a meeting house and refuge for the early Friends, which it remained until Fox's death in 1691, when a new meeting house was built nearby. William Penn visited Swarthmoor in 1676, and Fox wrote his famous Journal while staying there. Judge Fell died in 1658 and 11 years later George Fox married the judge's widow Margaret.

Today Swarthmoor Hall belongs to the Religious Society of Friends. It is a beautiful and atmospheric old house.

Well, I never knew this
about
SOUTH FURNESS

The SOUTH LAKES WILD ANIMAL PARK near Dalton-in-Furness is THE ONLY ZOO IN BRITAIN THAT PROVIDES A HOME FOR BOTH THE WORLD'S LARGEST TIGER, THE AMUR TIGER, and THE WORLD'S SMALLEST TIGER, THE SUMATRAN TIGER. It also boasts THE LARGEST COLLECTION OF KANGAROOS OUTSIDE AUSTRALIA.

The ULVERSTON CANAL, linking Ulverston with the sea at Morecambe Sands, and constructed with the aim of giving the isolated town a port, was built by Scottish engineer JOHN RENNIE and completed in 1796. Dead straight, it is just over 1 mile (1.6 km) long, 65 ft (20 m) wide and 15 ft (4.6 m) deep, THE SHORTEST, WIDEST AND DEEPEST CANAL IN BRITAIN. Ulverston ceased to be a port of any significance after the Second World War and the canal fell into disuse, but the seaside end makes a pleasant beauty spot, with an inn, a lock-keeper's cottage, some dilapidated lock gates and fine views across the sands. The canal itself now runs alongside a huge GlaxoSmithKline complex, fortunately well hidden by trees.

VICKERSTOWN on WALNEY ISLAND was begun in 1898, and laid out by Vickers as a model town for the ship workers from their Barrow ship-yards, along the lines of George Cadbury's Bourneville. Although the houses are now mostly privately owned, Vickerstown was declared a Conservation Area in 1988. Vickerstown is the model for the fictional VICARSTOWN from the Revd W. Awdry's *Thomas the Tank Engine* stories, while Walney Island was the inspiration for the ISLE OF SODOR where the engines lived.

CARTMEL PRIORY, the noblest church in Furness, dominates the small and delightful stone village of CARTMEL. The Augustinian Priory was founded in 1189 and although much rebuilt over the years is renowned for its glorious east window and for its extraordinary tower, which was extended in the 15th century with the new upper section not positioned squarely on the base, but instead rotated through 45 degrees – a feature FOUND NOWHERE ELSE IN ENGLAND. In a famous case in 1929 the Priory's rare 1596 first edition of SPENSER'S *FAERIE QUEENE* was stolen and offered for sale in New York. It was found quite impossible to sell and was later returned to the Priory. It is now in the library of Lancaster University.

CARTMEL RACECOURSE, while small, has THE LONGEST RUN-IN IN BRITAIN, at four furlongs. In 1974 the racecourse was the scene of the infamous 'GAY FUTURE COUP', in which an Irish betting syndicate attempted to defraud bookmakers by substituting horses and using various other means to disguise the true potential of Gay Future, and so lengthen the odds against his winning the race.

HOLKER HALL, near Cartmel, is the home of Lord and Lady Cavendish, members of the Duke of Devonshire's family. The property has never been sold since it was acquired by the Preston family at the Dissolution of the Monasteries in 1536, but has descended through inheritance and marriage. In the library can be seen a microscope belonging to the distinguished scientist HENRY CAVENDISH (1731–1810), who discovered hydrogen. LADY DOROTHY CAVENDISH, daughter of the 9th Duke of Devonshire and wayward wife of Prime Minister Harold Macmillan, was born at Holker Hall in 1900.

The gardens at Holker Hall have been described as 'amongst the best in the world' by the *Good Gardens Guide*, and include the HOLKER GREAT LIME, 72 ft (22 m) high and nearly 8 ft (2.4 m) in diameter, which dates from the 17th century and is one of BRITAIN'S 50 GREAT TREES.

The SOUTH NATURE RESERVE on Walney Island is home to THE LARGEST NESTING GROUND OF HERRING GULLS AND LESSER BLACK-BACKED GULLS IN EUROPE.

ULVERSTON claims to have INVENTED POLE-VAULTING AS A COMPETITIVE SPORT, by adapting the practice of the farmers of Arrad Foot who would leap over their farm gates using their shepherd's crooks. Ulverston's TOM RAY became WORLD POLE-VAULTING CHAMPION in 1887.

CONISHEAD PRIORY, 2 miles (3.2 km) south of Ulverston, is a Victorian Gothic fantasy, home since 1976 to the MANJUSHRI KADAMPA MEDITATION CENTRE, dedicated to the teaching of Buddhism and the art of Buddhist meditation. It is a remarkable place to find in the English Lake District, although it was originally founded in 1170 as a hospital, a place of rest and recuperation, not dissimilar to its function today. In the grounds can be found THE WORLD'S FIRST KADAMPA WORLD PEACE TEMPLE, opened in 1997, and the first in a projected series of international temples dedicated to world peace to be built in every major city in the world. Inside is THE LARGEST BUDDHA EVER CAST OUTSIDE THE ORIENT.

Windermere

The Roundhouse on Belle Isle, first round house ever built in Britain

Windermere

England's Largest Lake

Windermere is the largest natural lake in England, and the 16th largest in Britain, 10½ miles (16.9 km) long, just under 1 mile (1.6 km) wide and up to 219 ft (67 m) deep.

Boating

Windermere is the Lake District's busiest lake, with sailing, fishing, water sports, sightseeing and all kinds of passenger boats shuttling between Waterhead at the northern end of the lake, Lakeside at the southern end, and points in between. In previous

centuries boats transporting wool, fish, timber and the products of the area's slate and copper mines plied their trade from shore to shore.

The lake has for a long time been classified as a public highway and for some 500 years there has been a ferry service across the narrowest part of the lake, from Bowness to the opposite shore. In 1635 the ferry capsized during a storm, and 47 people and 11 horses returning from a wedding in Hawkshead were drowned.

In the early years of the 19th century, various enterprising fellows offered their services rowing people about the lake, and there was a sailing packet operated by White and Gibson of Ambleside for the better off.

All Steamed Up

In 1845 a paddle steamer named *LADY OF THE LAKE*, THE FIRST STEAMBOAT EVER TO OPERATE ON AN ENGLISH LAKE, was launched at Newby Bridge by the WINDERMERE STEAM YACHT COMPANY. The opening ceremony was boycotted by WILLIAM WORDSWORTH, who disapproved of the idea, worried that

Windermere might become swamped with tourists, but was attended by Windermere's answer to Coniston's John Ruskin, HARRIET MARTINEAU, England's first female sociologist and journalist (*see* Ambleside).

In 1847 a second company, THE WINDERMERE IRON STEAMBOAT COMPANY, was formed to run cruises for passengers of the new Kendal to Windermere Railway, and by 1850 they had two boats on the lake, *FIREFLY* and *DRAGONFLY*. These two boats were much faster than the *Lady of the Lake*, and whenever the *Dragonfly* overtook the old lady on the lake, the *Dragonfly's* band would strike up 'The Girl I Left Behind'. The two companies merged in 1858 to become the WINDERMERE UNITED YACHT COMPANY.

In 1869 the Furness Railway opened a branch line from Haverthwaite to Lakeside at the southern end of Windermere and by 1872 had taken over sole control of the Windermere United Yacht Company. The railways continued to run the steamers through all their incarnations, from London Midland Scottish to British Rail, until the 1980s, and today a private company, WINDERMERE LAKE CRUISES, operate the steamboats alongside modern launches.

The flagship of the Windermere fleet is the steamer *Tern*, launched in 1891 and the oldest steamboat operating on Windermere.

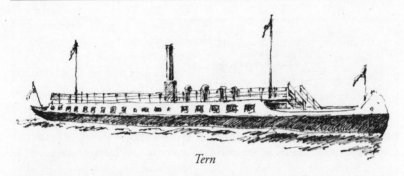

Tern

The historic headquarters of the Windermere Iron Steamboat Company is a beautiful Victorian cast-iron colonnaded structure at Lakeside, which is now used as the terminus of the Haverthwaite and Lakeside Railway.

Speed Records

On Friday 13 June 1930, racing driver SIR HENRY SEGRAVE, the FIRST MAN TO TRAVEL AT OVER 200 MPH (320 KPH), set a new world water speed record of 98.76 mph (158.90 kph) on Windermere, in *MISS ENGLAND II*. On his return run the boat hit a log and overturned, killing his mechanic, VICTOR HALIWELL, and badly injuring Segrave, who suffered a punctured lung. He was carried ashore to Belle Grange, a house on the western shore at High Wray, but died a few hours later. There is a debate about whether Segrave could be said to be the first man to officially hold both the world land speed record and the world water speed simultaneously, given that he was alive for only a short time after

achieving the latter, or whether that accolade should go to Donald Campbell, who held both records in the same year, 1964 (*see* Coniston). Segrave was certainly THE FIRST BRITON TO WIN A GRAND PRIX IN A BRITISH CAR, winning the French Grand Prix in a Sunbeam in 1923.

Between 1952 and 1972 NORMAN BUCKLEY, the owner of the Low Wood Hotel, set seven world water speed records on Windermere in boats he designed and built himself. One of his record-breaking boats, *MISS WINDERMERE IV*, launched in 1958, can be seen in the Windermere Steamboat Museum. Norman Buckley was an official timekeeper for Donald Campbell, and was present at Camp-

Old Boilers

The WINDERMERE STEAMBOAT MUSEUM lies on the lakeside just to the north of Bowness and tells the story of Windermere's unique boating heritage. Amongst the highlights of the museum's collection of steamboats are:

S.I. *DOLLY*, launched in 1850 and THE OLDEST MECHANICALLY POWERED BOAT IN THE WORLD, salvaged from the bottom of Ullswater in 1962.

T.S.S.Y. *ESPERANCE*, launched in 1869, THE OLDEST BOAT ON THE LLOYDS YACHT REGISTER and THE FIRST KNOWN TWIN-SCREW YACHT TO BE BUILT IN BRITAIN. Owned by HENRY SCHNEIDER, who built the ironworks at Barrow-in-Furness.

Esperance

S.S. *RAVEN*, launched in 1871, THE OLDEST VESSEL ON THE LLOYDS YACHT REGISTER STILL HAVING HER ORIGINAL MACHINERY.

bell's fatal record attempt on Coniston Water in 1967.

Galava

The remains of the Roman fort of GALAVA can be found in a field at Borrans Park by Waterhead, at the northern end of the lake, not far from the pier where visitors to Ambleside disembark. There was a wooden fort recorded here in about AD 80, but the ruins we see today come from a replacement stone fortification from the 2nd century. Galava was connected to the port at Ravenglass via the road that runs over the Hardknott Pass and by Hardknott Castle.

Windermere's Islands

Windermere possesses 18 islands, most of them called 'Holme', which is the Norse word for island. The largest of them is BELLE ISLE and the smallest is MAIDEN HOLME, which looks like little more than a single floating tree.

Belle Isle

BELLE ISLE, originally called Long Holme and then Great Island, lies in the centre of Windermere opposite Bowness, and is the largest of the islands on the lake, ¾ mile (1.2 km) long and covering 38 acres (15.4 ha). It is THE ONLY ISLAND ON THE LAKE EVER TO HAVE BEEN INHABITED, in the first instance by the Roman governor of Galava, who had a villa there.

Belle Isle was a Royalist stronghold during the Civil War in the mid 17th century, and came under fire from Parliamentarian COLONEL BRIGGS, who fired on it with cannon from Cockshott Point. The landowner ROBERT PHILIPSON was so incensed that he rode into Kendal and galloped up the aisle of the parish church during Evensong, brandishing his sword, intent on seeing the colour of Colonel Briggs's insides. In a fine example of the Church Militant the congregation rose up and overpowered him, forcing the gallant cavalier to flee, leaving behind his sword and helmet. These are displayed with pride in the church today.

Roundhouse

In 1774 the new owner of Belle Isle, Nottingham businessman Thomas English, started work on a new house for the island, inspired by the Villa Vincenza in Rome. It was THE FIRST ROUND HOUSE EVER BUILT IN ENGLAND. It cost him £5,000 and later drew withering scorn from William Wordsworth, who described it as a 'pepper-pot' in his poem 'The Prelude', although that was no surprise as the great poet seemed to disapprove of pretty much every new development in the Lake District. The Roundhouse suffered a disastrous fire in 1996 but has since been restored.

In 1781 the island was bought by JOHN CHRISTIAN CURWEN for his cousin and future wife ISABELLA CURWEN, and the name was changed to Belle Isle in her honour. The Curwens instigated regattas on the lake, and one of their sailing yachts, the *Margaret*, launched in 1780 and THE OLDEST CUMBRIAN-BUILT YACHT IN EXISTENCE, can be seen in the Steamboat Museum.

Later generations of Curwens were great friends with Wordsworth, despite his views on their island abode, and he became an enthusiastic spectator of the regattas.

HEN HOLME is used as a starting point for yacht races, and got its name from the hens that were kept there by two monks who lived in a chapel on Lady Holme, charged with praying for a local lord of the manor.

CROW HOLME used to be a kennel for the hounds of the Windermere Harriers.

LILIES OF THE VALLEY, East and West, were named after the wild lilies that used to grow on them, until picked to extinction by 18th-century tourists.

SILVER HOLME became Cormorant Island in Arthur Ransome's *Swallows and Amazons*.

Windermere (Town)

Wordsworth's Nightmare

The town of WINDERMERE, which is not actually quite on the lake, began life as three hamlets called Birthwaite, Applethwaite and Heathwaite, situated at the midpoint of the eastern shore. In 1847 the railway arrived from Kendal, wilfully disregarding the horrified protests of Wordsworth, whose poems extolling the beauties of the Lake District were the main reason so many people wanted to come here in the first place. It was decided to rename the three hamlets Windermere after the lake, so that potential visitors would more easily recognise the destination. As an ever-increasing number of tourists came to enjoy the glorious scenery, hotels began to spring up and Windermere rapidly expanded to merge with the much older Bowness.

Bowness-on-Windermere

BOWNESS-ON-WINDERMERE IS THE LARGEST TOWN WITHIN THE LAKE DISTRICT NATIONAL PARK. There has been a settlement on the site since Norse days, but the oldest surviving building in the town is the Old Rectory, which dates from the year of Agincourt, 1415. The tiny core of the old part of Bowness is down by the lake, a maze of little alleyways and streets that wriggle around the rectory and around St Martin's Church, built in 1483, restored in 1870. The beautiful east window of St Martin's contains medieval stained glass from Cartmel Priory, and includes a very early example of the stars and stripes, the arms of a 15th-century JOHN WASHINGTON from Lancashire, ancestor of the first President of the United States, George Washington.

A tombstone at the west end of the church commemorates the slave-trader JOHN BOLTON, who lived at STORRS HALL, while outside in the churchyard is a headstone with the following inscription:

> In memory of Rasselas Belfield,
> a Native of Abyssinia,
> who died on the 16th day of
> January 1822, aged 32 years.

> A Slave by birth I left my native land,
> And found my Freedom on
> Britannia's Strand.
> Blest Isle! Thou Glory of the
> Wise and Free,
> Thy Touch alone unbinds the
> Chains of Slavery.

Victorian Villas

As well as day-trippers, the railway brought rich businessmen from Lancashire who built themselves great summer villas overlooking the lake, most of which are now hotels.

STORRS HALL was built in 1811 for Sir John Legard, then became the home of a chap called JOHN BOLTON, who organised a huge regatta in 1825 attended by Wordsworth and Sir Walter Scott. Alas, Bolton's money came from the rum and slave trades, and it is thought that some of both were smuggled into the cellars of the hall along a secret passage from the lake. Legend has it that one of the slave girls put a curse on Storrs Hall to ensure that it should never pass from father to son – and indeed it never has. It is now a hotel.

BELSFIELD HOUSE, now the Belsfield Hotel, was the home of HENRY SCHNEIDER (1817–77), an owner of the Furness Railway and founder of the Barrow Steelworks, once the biggest steelworks in the world. Every day he would sail on his steamboat *ESPERANCE* to the railway station at Lakeside, partaking of breakfast on the way, and then take the train, on which he had a private carriage, to his office in Barrow. *Esperance*, which was

St Martins, Bowness

the model for Captain Flint's houseboat in Arthur Ransome's *Swallows and Amazons*, is now in the Steamboat Museum.

LANGDALE CHASE is an Elizabethan-style house built in 1891 for Mrs Edna Howarth, wife of a Manchester businessman. The house featured in Alfred Hitchcock's 1947 courtroom thriller *The Paradine Case*, and in the BBC's 1988 film about Donald Campbell, *Across the Lake*. It is now the Langdale Chase Hotel.

Langdale Chase

BROCKHOLE was built in 1895 by Dan Gibson for Manchester silk merchant William Henry Aldolphus Gaddum, whose wife was a cousin of Beatrix Potter. In 1969 it opened as the LAKE DISTRICT NATIONAL PARK VISITOR CENTRE, the FIRST SUCH NATIONAL PARK VISITOR CENTRE IN BRITAIN.

BROAD LEYS was built in 1898 and designed by the architect C.F.A. Voysey as a holiday home for businessman Currer Briggs from Leeds. According to Pevsner, Broad Leys was Voysey's masterpiece. It

is now the Windermere Motor Boat Club, and featured in the 1981 film *The French Lieutenant's Woman*, starring Meryl Streep and Jeremy Irons.

BLACKWELL is a supreme example of Arts and Crafts architecture. It was designed by M.H. Baillie Scott and built between 1897 and 1900 as a holiday home for Manchester brewer Sir Edward Holt. In 2000 the house was bought by the Lakeland Arts Trust and restored as a living museum of Arts and Crafts design. The White Drawing Room, which has stunning views of the lake, is a particularly gorgeous room.

Apart from Storrs Hall and Belsfield House, each of these splendid houses boasted gardens designed by THOMAS MAWSON (1861–1933), a Lancashire-born garden designer and landscape architect who moved into design after running a garden nursery in Windermere, and ended up as the first President of the Institute of Landscape Architects. He was especially renowned for his blending of architecture and nature. Although perhaps best remembered for his Lakeland gardens, which included those at Holker Hall and Graythwaite Hall in Furness, he also

laid out the Peace Palace Gardens at The Hague, in Holland, and the famous Pergola Gardens at The Hill, Lord Leverhulme's home on Hampstead Heath in London.

Kendal

'Auld Grey Town'

KENDAL IS THE LARGEST TOWN IN THE HISTORIC COUNTY OF WESTMORLAND, and the southern gateway to the Lakes. CATHERINE PARR, Henry VIII's sixth wife, and the only one to survive him, was born in 14th-century Kendal Castle in 1512. The ruins of the castle, up on a green hill above the town, are impressive, with extensive views.

HOLY TRINITY CHURCH, begun in the 13th century and added to in the 15th and 18th centuries, has five aisles and is THE WIDEST PARISH CHURCH IN ENGLAND, 103 feet (31.4 m) across.

The artist GEORGE ROMNEY had his first studio in Kendal, and lived his final years in the town, dying there in 1802. A number of his portraits hang in Kendal's Abbot Hall Art Gallery beside the church.

Kendal's most famous export, KENDAL MINT CAKE, was invented in 1869 by JOSEPH WIPER, a local confectioner, when he overcooked a recipe for glacier mints, and the mixture started to grain and become cloudy. When the liquid was poured from the pan and cooled, mint cake was the result. Wiper set up a factory and marketed his new treat, which was an instant success, particularly as a source of energy for climbers of the Lake District mountains. WIPER'S KENDAL MINT CAKE was supplied to Sir Ernest Shackleton's Antarctic expedition of 1914–16. ROMNEY'S KENDAL MINT CAKE, named after Kendal's own painter George Romney, was founded by another local confectioner called Sam T. Clarke in 1918, and was carried to the summit of Mount Everest in 1953 by the first men to conquer the world's highest mountain, Sir Edmund Hilary and Sherpa Tensing. Tensing left some mint cake at the top to appease the mountain gods.

Alfred Wainwright
(1907–91)

ALFRED WAINWRIGHT, 'patron saint of Lake District walkers', was born in Lancashire and first visited the Lakes when he was 23, on a walking holiday with his cousin.

A year later, in 1931, he married and moved to Kendal, where he lived for the rest of his life, serving for 20 years as Borough Treasurer. He would walk the fells alone almost every day, whatever the weather, and record his experiences, which eventually led to him putting together his *Pictorial Guide to the Lakeland Fells* in 1952. He completed one page per day, and over the next 13 years produced seven volumes, all with his own hand-drawn illustrations. They were originally written for his own interest, but Henry Marshall, Chief Librarian of Kendal and Westmorland, offered to publish them, and soon they were sold in local shops and appeared in local newspapers, becoming highly prized.

In the late 1960s Wainwright explored the Pennines in his *Pennine Way Companion*, and in 1973 he devised the Coast to Coast walk from St Bees on the Cumberland coast to Robin Hood's Bay in Yorkshire. Despite having no official designation, the Coast to Coast walk is enjoyed by thousands of devoted followers every year.

In the 1980s Wainwright appeared in *Wainwright's Walks* on television, along with presenter Eric Robson, and these walks are still repeatedly televised with new presenters to this day.

In line with his wishes, Wainwright's ashes were scattered on the shore of Innominate Tarn beneath the summit of HAYSTACKS, his favourite mountain, and there is a memorial tablet to him, in view of Haystacks, in the window of St James's Church in nearby Buttermere.

Levens Hall

Topping Topiary

LEVENS HALL IS THE LARGEST ELIZA-BETHAN HOUSE IN CUMBERLAND OR WESTMORLAND, and one of the most lovely houses in England. It was built around a 13th-century pele tower and added to in the 18th and 19th centuries. In 1688 the house was won from ADAM BELLINGHAM by his cousin COLONEL JAMES GRAHME, Keeper of the Privy Purse to James II, at a game of cards. The winning card was an ace of hearts, and in recognition of this the down spouts of the guttering are decorated with hearts.

The interior displays BRITAIN'S FINEST EXAMPLE OF SPANISH LEATHER WALL COVERINGS, and THE EARLIEST KNOWN ENGLISH PATCHWORK, dating from 1708 and executed by the Grahme daughters.

The gardens of Levens Hall contain THE OLDEST TOPIARY GARDEN IN THE WORLD. It was laid out in 1694 by Frenchman GUILLAUME BEAUMONT, a pupil of Le Nôtre at Versailles, and already well known in England for his work at Hampton Court Palace. The gardens at Levens, however, are the only surviving example of his work, and are almost exactly as he designed them over 300 years ago. They are an extravagant riot of box, beech and yew, cut into extraordinary shapes, with pyramids, columns and fancy displays with names like the 'Judge's Wig', the 'Bellingham Lion' and 'Queen Elizabeth and her Maids of Honour'. One exhibit, the 'Jugs of Morocco', highlights the powerful Morocco ale that is brewed to a secret Elizabethan recipe in the house kitchen, and was popular at the convivial annual

Radish Feast that was held in the grounds for 60 years during the 19th century.

Sizergh Castle

Inlaid Chamber and Largest Rock Garden

SIZERGH CASTLE, 4 miles (6.4 km) south of Kendal, has been the home of the Strickland family for nearly 800 years. Stricklands fought at Hastings, in the Wars of the Roses, at Agincourt and with Charles I at Edgehill. In 1950 the house was gifted to the National Trust but is still inhabited by the Stricklands.

The core of the medieval great hall is built around a huge 14th-century pele tower, flanked with Elizabethan wings, and the house was extended in Georgian style in the 1770s.

Sizergh is noted for its panelling, particularly that of the INLAID CHAMBER, where the sumptuous panels inlaid with English poplar and oak, which were restored at the Victoria and Albert Museum in London, have been returned to the room they originally graced, creating a warm, rich décor.

Sizergh's gorgeous rock garden is THE NATIONAL TRUST'S LARGEST LIMESTONE ROCK GARDEN.

Kirkby Lonsdale

Ruskin's View

KIRKBY LONSDALE, all timeless narrow streets and charming grey stone houses, perches above the River Lune, from which it derives its name (Lunesdale). The view across the Lune valley from the churchyard was the subject of a painting by Turner, which attracted John Ruskin to come and see the real thing for himself. He described it as 'one of the loveliest scenes in England, and therefore the world', and it is now known as 'Ruskin's View'.

ST MARY'S CHURCH is the finest Norman church in Westmorland, its nave supported by stout Norman pillars carved with diamonds like those in Durham Cathedral.

Spanning the Lune with three fine arches is DEVIL'S BRIDGE, built in the 12th century. The story goes that it was put there by the Devil at the request of an old woman who could not get across the fast-flowing river to retrieve her cow. All he asked for in return was the soul of the first living thing to cross the bridge. The old woman agreed, but instead of going across herself, as the Devil had anticipated, she threw a bun on to the bridge and her dog pursued it, straight into the arms of Beelzebub. A dog, according to folklore, has no soul, and so the Devil was left disappointed.

The girls' school at CASTERTON, 1 mile (1.6 km) up the road, was attended by the Brontë sisters, and was the model for Lowood School in Charlotte Brontë's *Jane Eyre*.

Well, I never *knew this*
about
WINDERMERE

The name WINDERMERE comes from the 10th-century Norse name 'Vinand's Mere'. Mere is the Old English for lake, and so to call it Lake Windermere is an unnecessary doubling up.

The viewpoint of ORREST HEAD, which rises to 784 ft (240 m) above the town of Windermere, was the first Lakeland height climbed by Alfred Wainwright, in 1930. There is now a plaque at the summit commemorating the place where he first fell in love with the Lake District.

BOWNESS-ON-WINDERMERE is the town of Rio in Arthur Ransome's *Swallows and Amazons*.

One of the most fascinating houses in the Lake District is TOWNEND, at the south end of Troutbeck village near Windermere. Here the visitor is struck immediately by the tall, sturdy chimneys, similar to those at Coniston Hall, but whereas Coniston was built for gentry, Townend is a splendid example of a farmhouse belonging to a prosperous yeoman farmer, in this case George Browne. Townend was

built in 1626 and remained in the Browne family for 11 generations until handed over to the National Trust in 1943. The house contains original oak furniture and woodwork, and a collection of domestic appliances and implements accumulated over the years. An ancient slate barn stands across the road.

HOLEHIRD, a Victorian house at Troutbeck Bridge, was built in 1865 by J.S. Crowther, architect of Manchester Cathedral, and sits in the middle of 10 acres (4 ha) of gardens owned by the LAKELAND HORTICULTURAL SOCIETY. Beatrix Potter stayed in Holehird with her parents during the summers of 1889 and 1895. The gardens are open to the public, but the house is not.

KENDAL was the home until 2003 of K-SHOES, now part of Clarks.

The village of LONGSLEDDALE, near Kendal, is the model for Greendale, where children's favourite POSTMAN PAT and his black and white cat have their postal round. Author JOHN CUNLIFFE lived in a cottage on Greenside in Kendal while writing the stories, and was partly inspired by the tales he overheard at his local post office.

ULLSWATER

ULLSWATER + DAFFODILS + PATTERDALE +
HELVELLYN + MARTINDALE + EUSEMERE

'A host, of golden daffodils,' WILLIAM WORDSWORTH

Ullswater

'. . . the happiest combination of
beauty and grandeur, which any
of the lakes affords'
WILLIAM WORDSWORTH

ULLSWATER vies with Derwentwater for
the accolade of 'most beautiful of the
English lakes', and is often compared
to Lake Lucerne in Switzerland. It is

THE SECOND LARGEST LAKE IN THE LAKE
DISTRICT, 7½ miles (12 km) long,
½ mile (800 m) wide and with a maximum depth of 205 ft (62 m). Ullswater
is fed by numerous becks running off
the central mountains, and is drained
by the River Eamont, which flows out
past Penrith and Brougham Castle to
join the River Eden.

ULLSWATER STEAMERS have been
plying the lake between Glenridding

and Pooley Bridge since 1855. One of their fleet, *LADY OF THE LAKE*, was launched in 1877 and is THE OLDEST WORKING PASSENGER VESSEL IN THE WORLD. In 1962 S.I. *DOLLY*, launched in 1850 and THE OLDEST SURVIVING MECHANICALLY POWERED BOAT IN THE WORLD, was salvaged from the bottom of Ullswater. It can today be seen in the Windermere Steamboat Museum.

In 1955 DONALD CAMPBELL broke the world water speed record on Ullswater, reaching 202.32 mph (325.53 kph) in his *Bluebird K7*.

Daffodils

I wandered lonely as a cloud
That floats on high o'er vales and hills,
When all at once I saw a crowd,
A host, of golden daffodils;
Beside the lake, beneath the trees,
Fluttering and dancing in the breeze.

On 15 April 1802, WILLIAM WORDS-WORTH and his sister DOROTHY were walking along the western shore of Ullswater after visiting Thomas Clarkson at Eusemere House (*see* page 105) when, as they were nearing LYULPH'S TOWER in the woods beyond GOWBARROW PARK, they came across a carpet of daffodils. As Dorothy wrote afterwards in her journal:

> 'I never saw daffodils so beautiful,
> they grew among the mossy stones
> about and about them, some rested
> their heads upon these stones as on
> a pillow for weariness, and the rest
> tossed and reeled and danced and
> seemed as if they verily laughed with
> the wind that blew upon them over
> the lake, they looked so gay ever
> dancing ever changing.'

Many believe that these were the daffodils that inspired William Wordsworth's most famous lines.

Today, alas, the exact spot is slightly spoiled by a main road and a car park, but daffodils still grow nearby, and compensation may be found in the delightful walk through the woods up to the waterfall, AIRA FORCE. On the way the path crosses a bridge that serves as a memorial to SIR CECIL SPRING-RICE (1859–1919), ambassador to the United States during the First World War, and author of the words to the hymn 'I Vow to Thee, My Country'.

wrecked on Duddon Sands. The elegant St Patrick's Church was designed by the Victorian architect Anthony Salvin, and replaces a 14th-century chapel. A large mound in the churchyard is all that remains of two famous yew trees that were over 600 years old when admired by Wordsworth, but were blown down by the storm that destroyed the Tay Bridge in 1879.

Patterdale

Yews, Astronomy and Lead

The tiny village of Patterdale sits right at the southern tip of Ullswater. The name Patterdale is a derivation of Patrick's Dale, and the saint is said to have performed baptisms at a well here during a visit to the area, after he had been ship-

Adam Walker
(1731–1821)

Adam Walker was born in Patterdale, the son of a woollen manufacturer who was too poor to send his son to school. Adam built himself a hut in the trees down by the river, where he would read in every available spare moment about philosophy, mathematics and all the sciences, until news of his scholarly nature spread and he was offered a position at a local school.

He later travelled throughout the country lecturing on experimental philosophy, and met Joseph Priestley, who introduced Walker to the members of the Lunar Society. Eventually Walker was able to set up lecture rooms in Hanover Square in London, and gave the most talked-about astronomical lectures of his day, illustrated by his own invention the Transparent

ORRERY or 'EIDOURANION'. This consisted of a back projection on to a large screen, using some hidden mechanism that demonstrated the motion of the Earth, the seasons, eclipses, tides and movements of heavenly bodies. A later refinement was special lighting and background music played on a 'CELESTINA', a type of glass harmonium Walker invented himself.

Walker's fellow Lakeland native and great friend George Romney painted a famous picture of Walker and his family, which Romney described as his 'favourite piece of friendship'. It now hangs in Beningbrough Hall in Yorkshire.

Glenridding

GLENRIDDING today is a terminus for Ullswater Steamers, and a starting point for the climb to the summit of Helvellyn via Striding Edge. The village developed originally to serve the GREENSIDE LEAD MINE in the hills above Patterdale.

Greenside Mine, THE BIGGEST LEAD MINE IN THE LAKE DISTRICT, opened in 1650 and was operational until 1962. At the end of the 19th century it became THE FIRST MINE IN THE WORLD TO USE ELECTRICITY TO POWER ITS WINDING GEAR, and was also THE FIRST MINE IN BRITAIN TO RUN AN ELECTRIC ENGINE UNDERGROUND.

Water for the water-wheels that originally provided the power for the mine was supplied by damming the nearby tarns, but more than once the dams broke, causing dreadful flooding in Glenridding. The Brown Cove Tarn dam is still intact, but water oozes through the bricks at the bottom and the structure is highly unstable – this is not as dangerous as it sounds as the tarn is now virtually empty of water.

Helvellyn

Third in Height

HELVELLYN is BRITAIN'S THIRD HIGHEST MOUNTAIN, and WESTMORLAND'S HIGHEST POINT at 3,118 ft (950 m). It is one of only four peaks in England over 3,000 ft (914 m). High above Red Tarn is the fearsome STRIDING EDGE, a slender, winding track along the top of a steep ridge that leads to the summit of Helvellyn. In places, it is less than 3 ft (0.9 m) wide, with an awesome drop on either side. In clement weather the route is relatively safe and the views are breathtaking, but when the wind blows and the cloud comes down, then Striding Edge becomes a perilous place.

In 1805 a young artist named CHARLES GOUGH fell to his death from the narrow path, and lay undiscovered for three months. His body

was finally located by a shepherd who was led to the spot by the sound of whimpering, and there he found Gough's faithful terrier FOXIE lying with her head on Gough's cold face, weak with hunger and sorrow, too feeble even to growl or wag her tail. The dog wouldn't be parted from her master even as his body was carried down the mountain, as if she was hoping still to hear his whistle and to scamper with him once again across the open windswept fells. Later that year Wordsworth brought his friends Humphry Davy and Sir Walter Scott to see the spot where Gough lay, and they were all greatly moved. Scott later wrote:

> How long didst thou think that his
> silence was slumber?
> When the wind waved his garment,
> how oft didst thou start?

In 1830 Edwin Landseer exhibited in the Royal Academy a painting of the scene, which he called 'Attachment'.

Martindale

Lonely but Lovely

High above the wooded eastern shore of Ullswater lies the Lake District's loneliest and loveliest church, ST MARTIN'S OF MARTINDALE. The tiny building marks the end of the winding single-track road: you can go no further – and why would you want to for this is a blessed place, ringed with green-gold hills and steeped in the peace of ages? There has been a church here since at least as far back as 1220, which was replaced by the present structure in 1634 – the date carved on the pulpit, once a two-decker.

The church is a single chamber with clear glass windows and wooden benches adapted from the old 17th-century box pews running along the walls. The font is Roman, carved from a stone shrine brought down 500 years ago from the Roman road of High Street at the head of the dale. There are marks on the side showing where the local people sharpened their tools

before the stone was hollowed out to use as a font.

In the churchyard stands a yew tree thought to be at least 800 years old. It watches over Lakeland's most secret spot. St Martin's was once the parish church of Martindale and full of life but the only people who come here today are loud, hearty walkers with boots and sticks, or gnarled explorers mad enough to persevere with the never-ending road.

About ½ mile (800 m) back is the new church of St Peter, which opened in 1881 – on the day it was consecrated the roof of old St Martin's fell in, as if in protest.

Observant visitors might be lucky enough to spot Martindale's herd of red deer, far away on the fells. It is THE OLDEST NATIVE HERD OF RED DEER IN ENGLAND.

Up a short bumpy track towards the head of the valley is a small building with a red roof known as the Bungalow, put there by the Earl of Lonsdale in 1910 as a hunting retreat for his friend the Kaiser, Wilhelm II (*see* Lowther).

Eusemere House

Goodness and Gannex

Sitting by a brook on the eastern shore of Ullswater, just below Pooley Bridge, and enjoying wide views of the lake,

is EUSEMERE HOUSE, a pretty stone cottage set in 34 acres (13.75 ha). It was built at the end of the 18th century for his retirement by the anti-slavery campaigner THOMAS CLARKSON (1760–1846). Clarkson came to live at Eusemere in 1796 with his new bride Catherine, exhausted by his seemingly fruitless struggles against the slave trade. Thomas and Catherine lived there for eight years, leading what one visitor called a 'bohemian peasant life' of farming and tending their garden. They received many distinguished visitors, including Sir Walter Scott, William Wordsworth and his sister Dorothy who became great friends of the couple, and Samuel Taylor Coleridge, who said of Clarkson, 'He, if ever human being did it, listened exclusively to his conscience, and obeyed its voice.'

In 1803 Catherine became ill and was advised to move to the warmer climes of Suffolk, where her father lived. Clarkson sold Eusemere and followed her in 1804, after first finishing the book he was writing, *Portraiture of Quakerism*, the first book to try and explain to the world the principles and peculiarities of the Society. Refreshed by his Lakeland sojourn, he rejoined the Abolition Committee, and once more took up arms against slavery. He later said that the years he spent in the Lake District surrounded by the beauties of nature, with time to reflect, had convinced him that the impulse that 'forced me into the great work' came from God.

Nearly 165 years later, in 1970, Eusemere House found fame again when it was purchased by LORD

KAGAN, inventor of the Gannex raincoat, as worn by his friend Prime Minister Harold Wilson, the Queen and the Duke of Edinburgh, US President Lyndon Johnson and Soviet leader Nikita Kruschev. Kagan spotted Eusemere from his private plane and bought it as a retreat – particularly welcome after he had served a ten-month prison sentence for tax evasion in 1980. Lord Kagan's family continued to own the house until his widow sold it in 2008.

Well, I never knew this about
ULLSWATER

The summit of the KIRKSTONE PASS on the way from Patterdale to Ambleside is 1,489 ft (454 m) above sea level, making it THE HIGHEST PASS OPEN TO TRAFFIC IN THE LAKE DISTRICT. The KIRKSTONE PASS INN, which stands near the summit, is THE THIRD HIGHEST PUB IN ENGLAND.

BROTHERS WATER is either THE LAKE DISTRICT'S SMALLEST LAKE or its LARGEST TARN.

Rugged and crookedly handsome, HARTSOP HALL near Brothers Water dates from the 16th century and was once the home of Sir John Lowther,

who became 1st Viscount Lonsdale. It is a glorious building to find in such majestic isolation and boasts beautiful windows, a fine oak staircase and a strange, hollowed-out priest hole. The Hall was extended in the 18th century rather imperiously across an ancient right-of-way, and there are tales of irate local farmers and shepherds who would resolutely stride right

through the house on their way to and from the fells.

PATTERDALE HALL, remodelled by Salvin, was in the 17th century the home of the Mounsey family, who earned the title KINGS OF PATTERDALE by defending the valley against a group of Scottish raiders in 1648. It is now an outdoor education centre.

The PATTERDALE TERRIER is a breed of small working dog that was first bred by farmers for hunting vermin in the Lake District in the 1920s.

A walk up Deepdale to the south of Patterdale village reaches GRIZEDALE TARN, where Wordsworth walked for the last time with his much-loved brother John, before John, who was a sea captain, drowned when his ship the *Earl of Abergavenny* went down off Portland Bill in 1805.

In the 19th century lead from the GREENSIDE MINE was shipped to America to make bullets used in the American Civil War.

The relatively flat summit of HELVEL-LYN provided a safe place for THE FIRST-EVER AEROPLANE LANDING ON A MOUNTAIN IN BRITAIN, in 1926. A plaque marks the spot and reads:

The first aeroplane to land on a mountain in Great Britain did so on this spot on December 22nd 1926. John Leeming and Bert Hinkler in an Avro 585 Gosport landed here and after a short stay flew back to Woodford.

THE FAR EASTERN LAKES

Clifton Hall overlooks the site of the last battle on English soil, fought in 1745

Clifton

The Last Battle

The small 12th-century church with a Norman door at CLIFTON is dedicated to St Cuthbert, and is built on one of the sites where the relics of the saint rested on their travels before finding peace at Durham.

The church and village of Clifton sit high on a hill above the Vale of Lowther, from where in December 1745 they overlooked the BATTLE OF CLIFTON MOOR, THE LAST BATTLE EVER FOUGHT ON ENGLISH SOIL. A group of Highlanders managed to hold up the pursuing Duke of Cumberland while the main Jacobite army escaped north across the Scottish border. Ten English dragoons who were killed at Clifton Moor are buried in the churchyard, and there is a simple commemoration stone to them near the gate.

Local legend points to a cottage

near the church where Bonnie Prince Charlie slept, or fretted, on the night before the battle, and from where he slipped away before dawn to lead his army to safety, leaving a handful of brave men to fight a gallant rearguard action.

Clifton Hall

In the farmyard next to the church there stands, in splendid isolation within its own little palisade, a 15th-century pele tower, all that remains of the once mighty CLIFTON HALL, home of the Wyberghs. Run by English Heritage, the tower is open to the public and provides a good insight into life in a fortified manor house, as well as time to reflect that when Jacobite soldiers were rummaging through these rooms and the clash of steel was heard for the last time in England, the United States of America didn't even exist.

Brougham

Ruined Castle, Rebuilt Medieval Hall, Two Churches

Brougham Castle

BROUGHAM CASTLE sits in a pleasant setting beside the River Eamont on the site of the Roman fort of Brocavum, and was begun by one of King John's knights, Robert de Vieux-

pont, in 1175. In 1268 the castle came into the hands of the Clifford family, with whom it remained for the next 400 years. Edward I stayed here in 1300 on his way to hammer the Scots.

Cliffords

The Cliffords were one of medieval England's most colourful families. They fought at Crécy and Poitiers; one was a founder of the Order of the Garter; another gave the news to Elizabeth I that the Armada was vanquished. Perhaps the most exceptional Clifford was Lady Anne Clifford (1590–1676), who at the age of 60, after a 30-year struggle for her rights, inherited the Clifford estates, and spent the next 26 years rebuilding her portfolio of castles and churches at Skipton, Pendragon, Appleby, Brough and here at Brougham. You can still see the room on the second floor of the keep where her father, the 3rd Earl of Cumberland, was born, and where she herself died in 1676.

Half a mile (0.8 km) away beside the busy A66, at the old gateway to the castle, is the COUNTESS PILLAR, a stone column topped with a sundial and gilded cupola, erected in 1656 by Lady Anne to mark the spot where she said a final goodbye to her mother, her staunch supporter in the long and bitter fight for her inheritance.

Brougham Hall

Standing in trees on a low hill overlooking the castle, BROUGHAM HALL is half castle and half country house, a Clifford home for less turbulent times. Most of it dates from Tudor days, and there is an impressive gatehouse and a circuit of walls that encloses an extensive courtyard. It also boasts a splendid door knocker of the same design as the sanctuary knocker at Durham Cathedral. The Hall was restored by Lady Anne, and so extended in Victorian times that it earned the title 'Windsor of the North'. In the 1950s the Hall was sold off to help ease the debt of the 4th Baron Brougham, and it no longer belongs to

the Brougham family, but there is an enthusiastic restoration plan afoot to restore what remains, and many of the rooms are now filled with craft shops and other enterprises.

St Wilfred's Chapel of Ease

ST WILFRED'S CHAPEL OF EASE, linked to Brougham Hall by a quaint bridge with iron gates, is long, low and buttressed and was built by Lady Anne Clifford to replace an earlier chapel. The interior is said to be sensational, a riot of medieval woodwork and carvings from the Continent installed by Lord Brougham in the 1840s. Both Sir John Betjeman and Sir Simon Jenkins wax lyrical about this Cumbrian treasure-house, and we must take their word for it, for the place is locked up tight, the impertinent casual visitor barred from its delights.

St Ninian, 'Ninekirks'

No such disappointments with Brougham's old parish church of ST NINIAN, known affectionately by the locals as Ninekirks,

which lies some 2 miles to the east of the castle. All it takes to revel in the treasures of this uniquely ravishing little church are sturdy boots, a map, and plenty of endurance. Ninekirks sits in a ring of trees in the middle of fields by a loop in the River Eamont at the end of a long, long track. The walk starts from a tiny car park that few will find and even fewer will make it into alive, for it lies hidden beside a long straight stretch of the A66 along which lorries speed implacably.

The walk, however, will soothe the most shredded of nerves, for it penetrates into deep countryside, above a beautiful looping river, with mountains in the distance. The track winds on and on and on until, long after you have forgotten why you came, the path suddenly dips into a green meadow, and there, on the far horizon, sitting in a profusion of wild flowers, is the sweetest church imaginable. If Lady Anne Clifford had left us nothing else she would be venerated for saving this Norman chapel, in her day the parish church and resting place of generations of de Broughams. 'It would in all likelyhood have fallen downe, it was soe ruinous, if it had not bin now repaired by me,' she claimed, and her initials AP (Anne Pembroke) and the date 1660 confirm this in plaster above the altar.

The interior is astonishing, filled by 17th-century box pews, with screens for the 'gentry' from the hall and castle, a wonderful double-decker pulpit complete with its canopy, or 'tester', rich panelling and the ancient gravestones of the de Broughams. To sit and drink in the wood fumes and the atmosphere of this uncommon place is rich reward for making it here.

Lowther

Castle

Lowther in thy majestic pile are seen
Cathedral pomp and grace in apt accord
With the baronial castle's sterner mien

Thus did Wordsworth describe LOWTHER CASTLE, standing in 3,000 acres (1,214 ha) of noble parkland, and approached by numerous avenues. Once the grandest house in Westmorland, it is now its most spectacular ruin. There have been many houses on this site, the seat of the Lowther family, now EARLS OF LONSDALE, since the days of Edward I. The present castle, a fine example of Gothic revival architecture, was completed in 1814, THE FIRST WORK OF ROBERT SMIRKE who went on to design the British Museum. The north front is 420 ft (128 m) long, almost wider than Westmorland, and the view from the tower stretches to the peaks of Helvellyn and Skiddaw – much of the land between belongs to the Lowthers, who remain to this day THE LARGEST LANDOWNERS IN THE LAKE DISTRICT.

At the end of the 19th century Lowther Castle was inherited by HUGH LOWTHER, 5TH EARL OF LONS-DALE (1857–1944), known variously as 'ENGLAND'S GREATEST SPORTING GENTLEMAN', 'LORDY' and the 'YELLOW EARL', the latter because of his love for the colour yellow. His bedroom, his cars, his servants' uniforms were all hues of yellow. Whenever he was resident in the castle the place would resound with the happy cries of royalty, politicians, sportsmen and artists, and the narrow lanes would be full of the Earl's fleet of yellow cars. Cars were a passion of the Yellow Earl's – he was THE FIRST PRESIDENT OF THE AUTOMOBILE ASSOCIATION (AA), which is why their vehicles are yellow. His greatest thrill was when the Kaiser arrived to stay at Lowther in a new Benz, driven by something never seen before in Westmorland – a chauffeur.

'England's Greatest Sporting Gentleman' loved hunting with the Kaiser, organised the first boxing match with gloves, introduced the Lonsdale Belt for boxing, and was PRESIDENT OF

ARSENAL FOOTBALL CLUB – which is why Arsenal's away strip is yellow.

'Lordy' was also a bon vivant who loved cigars and spent £3,000 a year on them. He is ONE OF ONLY TWO MEN – the other being Winston Churchill – TO HAVE A CUBAN CIGAR SIZE NAMED AFTER HIM: the LONSDALE CIGAR SIZE is 6 inches (15.2 cm) long with a 42 ring gauge.

The 5th Earl presided over grand days at Lowther, but they all came to an end with his death in 1957, after which the castle was abandoned, the roof and interiors were dismantled, and the family moved to Askham Hall across the river.

The Lowther Castle and Garden Project is engaged in restoring the castle so that it can be opened to the public.

Church

Not far from the castle stands ST MICHAEL'S CHURCH, on a high bluff looking over the river and the wooded grounds of Askham Hall to the mountains beyond. Saxon 'hog-back' gravestones have been found in the churchyard, and in the church porch is a Viking tombstone showing two warriors arriving at Valhalla by ship. The church was rebuilt in 1686 with rather unappealing 19th-century additions. The interior is stuffed with Lowther tombs as far as the eye can see. There are busts and statues and monuments: Lowthers at prayer, Lowthers in armour, Lowthers with wigs and pens and even skulls – no wonder the second Earl, who died in 1844, had to build his own extravagant mausoleum outside.

At the same time the church was rebuilt, the village next door was moved, and then moved again because it spoiled the view from the castle. The present village of Lowther, designed by Robert Adam, seems safe enough, having lasted for 200 years. Perhaps it has something to do with the LOWTHER OAK, a venerable, gnarled oak tree in the grounds which holds the fate of the Lowther family in its ancient branches – it is said that if the main branch ever touches the ground bad luck will strike the Lowthers, who have very sensibly propped the said branch up.

Well, I never knew this about

THE FAR EASTERN LAKES

HAWESWATER IS THE LAKE DISTRICT'S MOST EASTERLY LAKE. At 4 miles (6.4 km) long, just over ½ mile (800 m) wide and with a maximum depth of 200 ft (61 m), it is one of the larger lakes, and it was created from a smaller lake in the 1940s as a reservoir to serve Manchester. Construction of the

HAWESWATER DAM, THE FIRST HOLLOW BUTTRESS DAM IN THE WORLD, was begun in 1929 and the villages of Measand and Mardale were demolished and submerged. The remains of these villages can sometimes be seen when the water level is low. Haweswater is THE ONLY PLACE IN ENGLAND TO SEE GOLDEN EAGLES.

Tucked away down a lane in no-man's-land between the Lake District and Penrith is a hidden treasure, a Norman church standing alone on a circular

mound of prehistoric origins. ST MICHAEL'S, BARTON, has a low Norman tower and, inside, two extraordinary double chancel arches holding the tower up, quite unlike anything else to be seen in Lakeland. There are memo-

rials in the church to Wordsworth's grandfather Richard, who lived in nearby Sockbridge Hall and was buried here in 1760, to the poet's cousin John and his two wives, and to Wordsworth's aunt Anne, who married the curate at Barton. Almost a shrine.

SHAP is not only at THE HIGHEST POINT ON THE M6 but the site of the only abbey in Westmorland. Built by White Canons in 1200, Shap Abbey stands ½ mile (800 m) outside the village, in a lovely setting beside the River Lowther, and was probably THE LAST ABBEY TO BE FOUNDED IN ENGLAND. It was also thought to be THE LAST ENGLISH ABBEY TO BE DISSOLVED BY HENRY VIII, in 1540. There is in the village a cemetery specially built to receive bodies from the churchyard at Mardale, drowned by the waters of Haweswater in 1940.

Shap is halfway between Lands End and John o'Groats.

Lonely SLEDDALE HALL, a large farmhouse about 2 miles (3.2 km) west of Shap, featured in the 1986 film *Withnail and I* as Cow Crag, the Lake District cottage of Withnail's Uncle Monty.

The
North-Eastern Lakes

Carlisle Cathedral, the only English cathedral to have been
located in two different countries

Thirlmere

Ruskin's Regret

THIRLMERE, 3½ miles (5.6 km) long,
just over 1 mile (1.6 km) wide and up
to 158 ft (48 m) deep, was created in
1894 as a reservoir supplying Manchester. It was formed out of two smaller
lakes by the construction of a dam,
104 ft (31.7 m) high, at the north
end, and two villages, AMBOTH and
WYTHBURN, were drowned in the
process. The reservoir was opposed
by John Ruskin, who said that
'Manchester should be put at the
bottom of Thirlmere'.

A poignant reminder of Wythburn

is the proud little church at the south end of the valley, built in 1640 and restored in 1872, the crooked chancel half buried in the slope. Beside the telephone box outside the churchyard is a stone put there by Canon Rawnsley, which records two walks across Armboth Fells in July 1833 and 1843 that commenced from the church and inspired Matthew Arnold to write his poem 'Resignation'.

Penrith

My honoured mother,
she who was the heart
And hinge of all our learnings
and our loves

William and Dorothy Wordsworth's mother Ann was born in PENRITH, and both children attended the DAME ANNE BIRKETT SCHOOL overlooking St Andrew's Church. It was at the school that William met MARY HUTCHINSON, who would one day become his wife. Mary's parents are buried in the churchyard, as is Ann Wordsworth, in an unknown grave. Ann died when William was eight years old, but he always remembered her with great affection.

Dame Anne Birkett School

BONNIE PRINCE CHARLIE is reputed to have stayed in the GEORGE HOTEL in Penrith in 1745, when he passed through the town on his march to Derby during the second Jacobite Rising.

Greystoke

Private

GREYSTOKE CASTLE sits at the heart of THE LARGEST ENCLOSURE IN ENGLAND WITHOUT A ROAD OR PUBLIC RIGHT OF WAY RUNNING THROUGH IT, some 6,000 acres (2,430 ha).

There has been a castle at Greystoke since Llyulph de Greystoke built a wooden tower there in 1069. The present building, designed in Elizabethan style by Anthony Salvin, dates from 1868, and was badly damaged when used as a prisoner-of-war camp during the Second World War. It has now been restored. Greystoke has been home to 14 generations of the Howard family since the 4th Duke of Norfolk married the heiress Anne Dacre in 1571.

The massive, four-square church of St Andrew was built in 1255 and has a magnificent east window of medieval stained glass, second only to that of Carlisle Cathedral.

To the east of the village are three 'folly' farmhouses built in 1789 by the 11th Duke of Norfolk. Two of them,

FORT PUTNAM and BUNKERS HILL, are shaped like forts; the third, SPIRE HOUSE, resembles a church.

Caldbeck

D'ye ken John Peel with his coat so gray?
D'ye ken John Peel at the break of day?
D'ye ken John Peel when
he's far, far away?
With his hounds and his horns
in the morning?

CALDBECK is a neat granite village nestling among low fells right at the northern extremity of the Lake District. At first sight, all that is left of what was once a thriving industrial centre are a church, a few houses and a duck pond.

In the 17th and 18th centuries the 'cold beck' and its tributaries tumbling down off the hillside powered corn mills, woollen mills and even a brewery. A short walk from the church arrives at the HOWK, a rocky wooded glen where the remains of some of these enterprises dot the riverbank. Of particular interest is the BOBBIN MILL, which used to possess THE LARGEST WATERWHEEL IN ENGLAND, 3 ft (0.9 m) wide and 42 ft (12.8 m) in diameter.

An old corn mill below St Kentigern's Church, called the Priest's Mill, has been converted into a small arts and crafts centre, and has a restau-

Bobbin Mill

rant popular with visitors who come to see the grave of John Peel in the churchyard.

D'ye ken John Peel?

JOHN PEEL was born near Caldbeck in 1776, the son of a local horse-dealer. While still in his teens he eloped to Gretna Green with a local girl, Mary White, who bore him 13 children. A noble drinker, he became something of a local sight around the village in his long grey coat and knee-breeches, and his all-consuming pastime was hunting.

One evening he was sitting with his friend JOHN WOODCOCK GRAVES, reflecting on the day's hunting over a glass or two of something jolly, when Granny began singing the children to sleep upstairs. Graves snatched up his pen and started to jot down a ditty about his guest John Peel, using the tune Granny was humming, an old air called 'Bonnie Annie'. They spent the rest of the night singing it to each

other amidst howls of laughter, and as Peel was leaving, Graves slapped him on the back and cried, 'By Jove, John Peel, you'll be sung when we're both run to earth!'

He was right. John Peel died in 1854 at the age of 78 after falling off his horse, but the song 'D'ye ken John Peel' lives on and is still popular today, particularly in Cumberland. The version most people know was arranged by WILLIAM METCALFE, a choirmaster from Carlisle Cathedral, in 1868.

In 1977 a gang of anti-hunt protestors smashed up the headstone on John Peel's grave, dug a hole and left a fox's head in it. His remains were left undisturbed and the tomb has been carefully watched ever since.

Also buried in the churchyard is MARY HARRISON, better known as Mary Robinson, the celebrated 'Beauty of Buttermere' (see Buttermere).

Hutton-in-the-Forest

The Green Knight's Castle?

HUTTON-IN-THE-FOREST is a fantastical fairytale country house on the northern fringes of the Lake District near Penrith, whose architecture spans six centuries. The earliest structure is a pele tower of about 1350. The gallery, originally built over an open arcade, dates from 1630; then there is a gorgeous Frenchified Renaissance façade of 1685, which is sandwiched between the pele tower and a Victorian tower of 1830 by Anthony Salvin. The rather plain

south front is early 19th century and was castellated by Salvin at the same time as his tower. The newest piece is the Gladstone Tower, built as 'my gift to the old house' by Lady Vane (Margaret Gladstone) in 1886. The whole effect is exhilarating.

The house, which stands in deep forest woods, is the home of Lord and Lady Inglewood, and has been in their family since 1605. Before that, however, in the days of King Arthur, some say it was the Green Knight's castle in the tale of Sir Gawain and the Green Knight. Such is the magic of this place, seen in the right light, that the idea doesn't seem all that far-fetched ...

Carlisle

CARLISLE is often called the northern gateway to the Lake District.

The bluff on which Carlisle's castle now stands has been occupied since

Roman times, when there was a settlement here serving Hadrian's Wall. Variously described as the 'last town in England' or the 'first town in Scotland', Carlisle was fought over by the Scots and the English right up until the Jacobite rising of 1745, when Bonnie Prince Charlie, on his flight back to Scotland, left troops in Carlisle Castle so that he could be said to occupy at least one English town. The Jacobite troops were swiftly overwhelmed by the pursuing Hanoverians in THE LAST-EVER SIEGE OF AN ENGLISH CASTLE, and were imprisoned in the castle dungeons, where it is still possible to see the 'licking stones' which the prisoners licked at to obtain moisture.

The Market Cross marks the spot where Carlisle held its first fair in 1353, after being granted a charter by Edward III. In 1745 Bonnie Prince Charlie stood by this cross to proclaim his father King.

CARLISLE CATHEDRAL, the SECOND SMALLEST ENGLISH CATHEDRAL after Oxford, is THE ONLY ENGLISH CATHEDRAL TO HAVE BEEN LOCATED IN TWO DIFFERENT COUNTRIES. It was founded as a priory by William II and given to the Augustinian Black Canons by Henry I in 1122. The monks rather annoyingly owed their allegiance to the Bishop of Glasgow, and so in order to make Carlisle an exclusively English town, Henry created the See of Carlisle and made the prior a bishop.

Thus Carlisle is also THE ONLY CASE OF AN AUGUSTINIAN PRIORY BECOMING AN ENGLISH CATHEDRAL.

Carlisle Cathedral has suffered badly from the ravages of war and neglect, and there is precious little left of the Norman nave other than some strangely misshapen arches, which were warped by a drought in the 13th century when the ground on which they stand settled unevenly. The Early English chancel, though, is glorious, and the huge DECORATED EAST WINDOW is THE LARGEST IN ENGLAND after the Crécy Window in Gloucester Cathedral.

Dalemain

Bits and Pieces

DALEMAIN is not quite what it seems. There are no grand gates or manicured lawns to announce its presence; it just appears out of the trees like a

pink jewel in a bed of green. Behind the quite gorgeous blushing Georgian façade, which glows against the deep gold backdrop of fell and wood, lies a much older house based on a pele tower from the 12th-century days of Henry II. To this was added a 14th-century hall, two Elizabethan wings and finally the wonderful rosy front of 1744, all helping to create the magical, topsy-turvy family house which it still is today.

The fact that the pele tower belonged to John de Morville, brother of Hugh de Morville, one of the four knights who murdered St Thomas à Becket in Canterbury Cathedral, only heightens the thrill of Dalemain. In 1679 the house came to Sir Edward Hasell, 'Chiefe Officer' to Lady Anne Clifford, and the Hasells have owned it ever since.

The gardens are particularly noted for their trees, which include a 200-year-old Tulip Tree and THE LARGEST GREEK FIR TREE IN BRITAIN.

Well, I never knew this about

THE NORTH-EASTERN LAKES

ENGLAND'S FIRST PILLAR BOX was erected on CARLISLE'S BOTCHERGATE in September 1853.

In 1307 EDWARD I held his last parliament in Carlisle Cathedral before riding away on a white horse to inflict further punishment on the Scots of Robert the Bruce. He made it to the windswept marshes of BURGH-BY-SANDS on the Solway Firth, just south of the border by Hadrian's Wall, and died there in the arms of his loyal earls. Today a lonely monument stands tall in the fields, far from the road, on the bleak spot where Edward, Hammer of the Scots, breathed his last. A plaque at its base, put there in 1685 reads:

> Edward I fought a long bitter
> campaign to conquer Scotland
> Old and sick he made camp
> on these marshes whilst
> Preparing to subdue his
> enemy Robert the Bruce
> Edward died here on Jul 7 1307

It is a melancholy yet strangely moving place, imbued with the defiant spirit of a dying king.

In 1918 the 28th President of the United States of America, WOODROW WILSON, visited CARLISLE to see No. 83 Warwick Road, the house where his mother was born in 1826. Janet Woodrow was the fifth child of the Revd Thomas Woodrow and his wife Marion. The Revd Woodrow was a Scottish Presbyterian minister from Paisley, and THE FIRST OF HIS FAMILY TO LEAVE SCOTLAND IN 500 YEARS.

EDDIE STOBART's haulage company was founded in CARLISLE in 1970. He named his first truck after the model Twiggy, and ever since each new truck has been given a woman's name. Stobart insists that each of his distinctive green lorries is kept spotlessly clean and that his drivers wear ties at the wheel.

CARR'S WATER BISCUITS were founded in CARLISLE in 1831. Now 43 million packets of the popular biscuits are produced every year, and there was panic in the shops when floods in 2005 temporarily halted production.

Today, CARLISLE is THE MOST NORTHERLY CITY IN ENGLAND. However, it does not appear in the Domesday Book of 1086 because at that time it was part of Scotland.

The CARLISLE RACING BELLS date from around 1580 and are THE OLDEST KNOWN HORSE-RACING PRIZES IN BRITAIN.

Gazetteer

Interesting locations and places open to the public.

THE CENTRAL LAKES

DOVE COTTAGE & WORDSWORTH MUSEUM

Grasmere LA22 9SH
  Tel: 01539 435544
  www.wordsworth.org.uk

RYDAL MOUNT

Rydal, Near Ambleside,
  Cumbria LA22 9LU
  Tel: 01539 433002
  www.rydalmount.co.uk

THE NORTH-WESTERN LAKES (RIVER DERWENT)

HONISTER SLATE MINE

Honister Pass, Borrowdale, Keswick,
  Cumbria CA12 5XN
  Tel: 01768 777230
  www.honister-slate-mine.co.uk

DERWENT ISLAND HOUSE NT

Derwent Island, Lake Road,
  Keswick, Cumbria CA12 5DJ
  Tel: 01768 773780
  www.nationaltrust.org.uk

CUMBERLAND PENCIL MUSEUM

Main Street, Keswick,
  Cumbria CA12 5NG
  Tel: 01768 773626
  www.pencilmuseum.co.uk

MIREHOUSE

Mirehouse, Underskiddaw, Keswick,
  Cumbria CA12 4QE
  Tel: 01768 772287
  www.mirehouse.com

CARS OF THE STARS MUSEUM

Standish Street, Keswick,
  Cumbria CA12 5LS
  Tel: 01768 773757
  www.carsofthestars.com

FORCE CRAG MINE EH

www.english-heritage.org.uk

WHINLATTER FOREST PARK

Tel: 0845 3673787
www.forestry.gov.uk/whinlatter
forestpark

THE NORTH-WESTERN LAKES (RIVER COCKER)

JENNINGS BREWERY

Castle Brewery,
Cockermouth CA13 9NE
Tel: 0845 129 7190
www.jenningsbrewery.co.uk

WORDSWORTH HOUSE

Main Street, Cockermouth,
Cumbria CA13 9RX
Tel: 01900 820884
www.nationaltrust.org.uk

THE LAKELAND COAST

ST JAMES'S CHURCH, WHITEHAVEN

High Street, Whitehaven CA28 6HY
Tel: 01946 599485
www.whitehavenparish.co.uk

ST BEES PRIORY

St Bees, Cumbria CA27 0DR
Tel: 01946 822279
www.stbeespriory.org.uk

CALDER ABBEY

c/o Egremont Tourist Centre

Tel: 07092 031 363 or 01946 824052
www.calderabbey.co.uk

SELLAFIELD VISITOR CENTRE

Tel: 01946 727027
www.sellafieldsites.com

RUM STORY

Lowther Street, Whitehaven,
Cumbria CA28 7DN
Tel: 01946 592933
www.rumstory.co.uk

THE WESTERN LAKES

MUNCASTER CASTLE

Muncaster, Ravenglass,
Cumbria CA18 1RQ
Tel: 01229 717614
www.muncaster.co.uk

WORLD OWL CENTRE

Muncaster Castle, Ravenglass,
Cumbria CA18 1RQ
www.owls.org

WALLS CASTLE, RAVENGLASS EH

www.english-heritage.org.uk

RAVENGLASS AND ESKDALE RAILWAY

Station Hill, Main Street,
Ravenglass, Cumbria CA18 1SQ
Tel: 0845 000 0125
www.ravenglass-railway.co.uk

Eskdale Mill

Boot, Eskdale, Holmrook,
   Cumbria CA19 1TG
   Tel: 01946 723335
   www.eskdalemill.co.uk

CONISTON

Gondola Steamboat NT

Coniston Pier, Lake Road,
   Coniston, Cumbria LA21 8AN
   Tel: 01539 441288
   www.nationaltrust.org.uk

Brantwood

Coniston, Cumbria LA21 8AD
   Tel: 01539 441396
   www.brantwood.org.uk

Ruskin Museum

Coniston, Cumbria LA21 8DU
   Tel: 01539 441164
   www.ruskinmuseum.com

NORTH FURNESS

The Courthouse, Hawkshead NT

Hawkshead and Claife, near
   Hawkshead, Ambleside, Cumbria
   Tel: 01539 447997
   www.nationaltrust.org.uk

Hawkshead Grammar School

Tel: 01539 436735.
www.hawksheadgrammar.org.uk

Beatrix Potter Gallery NT

Main Street, Hawkshead,
   Cumbria LA22 0NS
   Tel: 01539 436355
   www.nationaltrust.org.uk

Wray Castle NT

www.nationaltrust.org.uk

Hill Top NT

Near Sawrey, Hawkshead,
   Ambleside, Cumbria LA22 0LF
   Tel: 01539 436269
   www.nationaltrust.org.uk

The World of Beatrix Potter

Bowness-on-Windermere,
   Cumbria LA23 3BX
   www.hop-skip-jump.com

Grizedale Forest

Grizedale, Hawkshead, Ambleside,
   Cumbria LA22 0QJ
   Tel: 01229 860373
   www.forestry.gov.uk/grizedalehome

The Lakeside and Haverthwaite Railway

Haverthwaite Station, Nr Ulverston,
   Cumbria LA12 8AL
   Tel: 01539 531594
   www.lakesiderailway.co.uk

SOUTH FURNESS

DALTON CASTLE NT

Market Place, Dalton-in-Furness,
   Cumbria LA15 8AX
   Tel: 01524 701178
   www.nationaltrust.org.uk

FURNESS ABBEY EH

Tel: 01229 823420
www.english-heritage.org.uk

PIEL CASTLE EH

Piel Island, Barrow-in-Furness,
   Cumbria
   Tel: 07798 794550 or 07516 453784
   www.english-heritage.org.uk

LAUREL AND HARDY MUSEUM

Brogden Street, Ulverston, Cumbria
   Tel: 01229 582292
   www.laurel-and-hardy.co.uk

SWARTHMOOR HALL

Swarthmoor Hall Lane, Ulverston,
   Cumbria LA12 0JQ
   Tel: 01229 583204
   www.swarthmoorhall.co.uk

SOUTH LAKES WILD ANIMAL PARK

Crossgates, Broughton Road, Dalton-
   in-Furness, Cumbria LA15 8JR
   Tel: 01229 466086
   www.wildanimalpark.co.uk

CARTMEL PRIORY

Tel: 01539 536536
www.cartmelpriory.org.uk

HOLKER HALL

Cark-in-Cartmel, Grange-over-Sands,
   Cumbria LA11 7PL
   Tel: 01539 558328
   www.holker.co.uk

WINDERMERE

WINDERMERE STEAMBOAT MUSEUM

Rayrigg Road, Windermere,
   Cumbria LA23 1BN
   Tel: 01539 445 565
   www.steamboats.org.uk

LAKE DISTRICT NATIONAL PARK VISITOR CENTRE

Lake District Visitor Centre at
   Brockhole, Windermere,
   Cumbria LA23 1LJ
   Tel: 01539 446601
   www.lakedistrict.gov.uk

BLACKWELL, THE ARTS & CRAFTS HOUSE

Bowness-on-Windermere,
   Cumbria LA23 3JT
   Tel: 015394 46139
   www.blackwell.org.uk

Museum of Lakeland Life

Abbot Hall, Kendal,
   Cumbria LA9 5AL
   Tel: 01539 722464
   www.lakelandmuseum.org.uk

Levens Hall

Kendal, Cumbria LA8 0PD
   Tel: 01539 560321
   www.levenshall.co.uk

Sizergh Castle NT

near Kendal, Cumbria LA8 8AE
   Tel: 01539 560951
   www.nationaltrust.org.uk

Townend NT

Troutbeck, Windermere,
   Cumbria LA23 1LB
   Telephone: 01539 432628
   www.nationaltrust.org.uk

ULLSWATER

Aira Force NT

www.nationaltrust.org.uk

Ullswater Steamers

The Pier House, Glenridding,
   Cumbria CS11 0US
   Tel: 01768 482229
   www.ullswater-steamers.co.uk

THE FAR EASTERN LAKES

Clifton Hall EH

Clifton Hall, Cumbria CA10 2EA
   www.english-heritage.org.uk

Brougham Hall

Tel: 01768 868184
www.broughamhall.co.uk

Brougham Castle EH

Middlegate, Penrith, Cumbria CA10 2AA
   Tel: 01768 862 488
   www.english-heritage.org.uk

THE NORTH-EASTERN LAKES

Hutton-in-the-Forest

Penrith, Cumbria CA11 9TH
   Tel: 01768 484449
   www.hutton-in-the-forest.co.uk

Carlisle Castle EH

Tel: 01228 591922
   www.english-heritage.org.uk

Carlisle Cathedral

7 The Abbey, Carlisle CA3 8TZ
   Tel: 01228 548 151
   www.carlislecathedral.org.uk

Dalemain

Penrith, Cumbria CA11 0HB
   Tel: 01768 486450
   www.dalemain.com

Index of People

Index of Places

Acknowledgements

My thanks as always to the home team at Ebury: Publishing Director Carey Smith, Senior Editor Imogen Fortes, the wonderful Sales and Publicity teams and editor Steve Dobell.

Special thanks to my agent Ros.

Thanks also to the weather, which was gorgeous.

Mai – you inspire me to climb the highest mountains.

I NEVER KNEW THAT ABOUT IRELAND

Bestselling author Christopher Winn takes us on a fascinating journey around Ireland, to discover the tales buried deep in the country's history. This book visits each of the four provinces – Ulster, Leinster, Munster and Connaught – and unearths the hidden gems that each county in these provinces holds. You'll be able to visit the holy mountain, Croagh Patrick in Country Mayo, where St Patrick is said to have driven all the snakes in Ireland into the sea. At Lismore Castle in County Waterford you will uncover the bathroom dedicated to Fred Astaire, whose sister Adele was the hugely popular Chatelaine of Lismore in the 1930s and 40s. On the winter solstice you can bathe in the sunlight that fills the burial chamber at Newgrange, County Meath – the oldest solar observatory in the world. This irresistible compendium of facts and stories will give you a captivating insight into the people, ideas and events that have shaped the individual identity of every place you visit.

£9.99   ISBN 9780091910259

I NEVER KNEW THAT ABOUT THE IRISH

In this charming book bestselling author Christopher Winn turns his attention to the Irish people, taking us on an enthralling journey around their homeland, discovering en route the intriguing and surprising ways the places and their history contribute to the Irish character. From County Leitrim, the most sparsely populated county in the Republic of Ireland to County Louth, Ireland's smallest county, discover the site of the first play performed in the Irish language, sail the longest navigable inland waterway in Europe and watch the horse racing at Ireland's first all-weather racecourse. Illustrated throughout with enchanting pen and ink drawings and packed with entertaining stories and astonishing facts, *I Never Knew That About the Irish* will entertain the whole family for hours on end.

£9.99   ISBN 9780091926748

I NEVER KNEW THAT ABOUT WALES

Packed full of legends, firsts, birthplaces, inventions and adventures, *I Never Knew That About Wales* visits the thirteen traditional Welsh counties and unearths the hidden gems that they each hold. You'll be able to visit Britain's smallest city, St David's, with its glorious 12th-century cathedral slumbering in a sleepy hollow near the sea. Explore Britain's greatest collection of castles from the first stone fortress at Chepstow to Britain's finest concentric castle at Beaumaris and the magnificent Caernarvon, birthplace of the first Prince of Wales. Browse through the second hand book capital of the world, Hay-on-Wye, wander the glorious Gower peninsula, Britain's first Area of Outstanding Natural Beauty. Take a trip to Fishguard, where the last invasion of Britain took place in 1797. Marvel at Thomas Telford's Menai Bridge, the world's first iron suspension bridge, or Pont-cysyllte, the longest bridged aqueduct in Britain.

£9.99   ISBN 9780091918583

**Order this title direct from
www.rbooks.co.uk/christopherwinn**

I NEVER KNEW THAT ABOUT LONDON

Bestselling author Christopher Winn takes us on a captivating journey around London to discover the unknown tales of our capital's history. See the Chelsea river views that inspired Turner in his final years and find out where London's first nude statue is. Explore London's finest country house in Charlton and unearth the secrets of the Mother of Parliaments. Spy out the village that gave its name to a car and the Russian word for railway station. Discover which church steeple gave us the design of the traditional wedding cake, where the sandwich was invented and where in Bond Street you can see London's oldest artefact. Visit the house where Handel and Jimi Hendrix both lived. Climb the famous 311 steps of the Monument, go from East to West and back again at Greenwich and fly the world's biggest big wheel. Brimming with stories and snippets and providing a spellbinding insight into what has shaped our capital, this beautifully illustrated gem of a book is guaranteed to inform and amuse in equal measure.

£9.99   ISBN 9780091918576

**Order this title direct from
www.rbooks.co.uk/christopherwinn**

I NEVER KNEW THAT ABOUT YORKSHIRE

In Britain's largest county, bestselling author Christopher Winn uncovers the hidden places, legends, secrets and fascinating characters of this unique and compelling piece of England. From England's largest vale and northern Europe's largest gothic cathedral to Britain's oldest city, Yorkshire is home to some of Britain's best architecture, most ravishing scenery and is the cradle of some of our country's most influential and individual characters. You will discover the only clog factory in the world, the first English actor to win an Oscar, the world's oldest association football club and largest expanse of medievel stained glass. This gem of a book will act as a wonderfully surprising and highly entertaining guide to one of England's best loved counties.

£9.99   ISBN 9780091933135

Order this title direct from
www.rbooks.co.uk/christopherwinn

I NEVER KNEW THAT ABOUT BRITAIN:
THE QUIZ BOOK

Bestselling author and quiz master Christopher Winn is here to test your knowledge of Britain with over 1000 questions to perplex and puzzle about our glorious islands. Covering a myriad of subjects including history, cathedrals, sports, records, modern Britain, royalty, people, places, deeds, discoveries and disasters, there is something to test everyone from Britain's brainiest boffins to the quiz beginner.

I Never Knew That About Britain: The Quiz Book features a range of questions from multiple choice teasers and odd ones out to picture quizzes illustrated with charming line drawings to test your knowledge of the famous faces and façades of Britain. Alongside these sit cryptic and puzzle quizzes plus special features spotlighting different regions so you can see just how well you know your local area.

Perfect for all ages, it will provide hours of entertainment and education for the whole family and have you proclaiming: 'I bet you never knew that!'

£9.99   ISBN 9780091933043

**Order this title direct from
www.rbooks.co.uk/christopherwinn**